P9-DVI-499

"Like a folk story . . . a fable about a man who settles into a pure and enduring peace, written by a man who believes that no such peace is possible . . . It's this that gives the book its clearest quality: wistfulness. If only Joseph's story could happen! the author seems to be saying."

Anne Tyler
The Baltimore Sun

"Singer's characters have old-fashioned beliefs, and they live by the grace of God rather than by the good offices of a psychoanalyst."

The Houston Chronicle

"The magical quality of Isaac Bashevis Singer's storytelling is once again evident in his latest novel, a long anecdote of a sinner's quest for grace. . . . Singer speaks to Jewish identity and conflict . . . with a sparkling twinkle in a moral tale that provides impish, comic relief."

Publishers Weekly

Fawcett Crest Books
by Isaac Bashevis Singer

ISAAC BASHEVIS SINGER

THE PENITENT

FAWCETT CREST • NEW YORK

A Fawcett Crest Book
Published by Ballantine Books
Copyright © 1983 by Isaac Bashevis Singer

Library of Congress Catalog Card Number: 83-8977

ISBN 0-449-20612-2

This edition published by arrangement with Farrar Straus & Giroux

Printed in Canada

First Ballantine Books Edition: February 1985
Third Printing: July 1988

THE
PENITENT

In 1969 I had my first opportunity to catch a glimpse of the Wailing Wall, about which I had heard so much. It looked somewhat different from the Wailing Wall carved on the wooden cover of my prayer book. That one showed cypresses, but I didn't see any trees here. Jewish soldiers guarded the entrance way. It was daytime and a crowd of Jews of all kinds had gathered. There were Ashkenazic and Sephardic. Youths with earlocks hanging to their shoulders, wearing knee-length breeches, rabbinical hats, and low shoes, spoke among themselves in a Hungarian Yiddish. A Sephardic rabbi dressed in white and surrounded by a circle of the curious preached in Hebrew about the Messiah. Some visitors recited the mourner's prayer, and others chanted the Eighteen Benedictions; some wound phylacteries around their arms, others swayed over the Book of Psalms. Everyone wore skullcaps, even those who were clean-shaven. Beggars held out hands for alms, some even haggling with their benefactors. The Almighty conducted business here on a twenty-four-hour basis.

I stood and looked at the Wall, and at the surrounding streets, which were inhabited by Arabs. The houses seemed to stand as if by a miracle, one looming over the next and leaning out and jostling for a better view of the stone wall that stood as a memento of the Holy Temple. The sun blazed with a dry heat and everything smelled of the desert, of ancient destruction, and of Jewish eternity.

Suddenly a little man in a long gaberdine and a velvet hat came up to me. Through the gaping front of his coat one could see a wide ritual garment with fringes that hung nearly to the knees. He had a whitish beard but a young face, with eyes black as cherries. They bore witness that he was a young man who had grayed early.

"I knew that you would come here," he said.

"You knew?"

"If you come here every day you're bound to meet everyone you want to sooner or later. The Wall is like a magnet that draws Jewish souls. Peace be with you."

And he shook my hand as rabbis do, softly, without pressure.

"I still don't know who you are," I said.

"How could you? When his brothers sold Joseph, he didn't have a trace of beard yet, that's why they didn't recognize him later. The last time you saw me I was clean-shaven. Now I'm a Jew like a Jew should be, thank God."

"A penitent, eh?" I used the words *baal tshuvah*.

"*Baal tshuvah* means one who returns. I came back home. So long as Jews were real Jews, only the body was in exile, not the soul. But when the Jews cast off their spiritual yoke, the body became emancipated and the soul went into exile. Oh, was that an exile—a bitter exile!"

"I still don't know your name."

"My name happens to be Joseph. Joseph Shapiro."

"A good Jewish name. Where did we meet?"

"Where didn't we? Whenever you lectured in New York, I was in the audience. I was a fervent disciple of yours.

True, you didn't know me. I had to introduce myself to you each time anew. But I knew you. I read everything you wrote. Here, I've stopped reading all that wordly stuff. But I occasionally still glance into a Yiddish newspaper and I see your name. At my age I became a yeshiva student here. We study the Gemara, the Tosaphot, other commentaries. Only now when I'm studying the Torah do I see what I've been missing all these years. Well, praised be God that we've met. How long will you be staying in Jerusalem? Where are you staying? You once wrote that you like to hear stories. I have a story for you, something unusual.''

We agreed that he should come to my hotel the following day. I invited him for lunch, but he didn't believe hotel kitchens were strict enough in their observance of the dietary laws.

The next day precisely at three he knocked on my door. I had ordered fruit and cookies for him. He sat down on the sofa and I took a seat on a chair. This is what Joseph Shapiro told me.

The
First
Day

1

Where shall I begin? First of all, let me tell you about my-self. You should know that I'm a member of a rabbinical family, descended from holy Jews. On my mother's side I stem from Shabbetai Cohen and whoever stems from Shab-betai Cohen also stems from Rabbi Moshe Isserles, from Rashi, and from King David himself. At least, that's what the genealogical specialists say. But what does it matter? I was in Poland in 1939 when the Nazis, may their name be blotted out, bombed Warsaw. I fled with other Jews over the Praga Bridge and went on foot to Bialystok. Although my beard is white, I'm a few years younger than you. I won't tell you my whole life story, it would take too long. I wandered through Russia, I starved, I slept in train depots, I suffered the whole gamut of troubles. Afterward, in 1945, I smuggled myself out of Stalin's land and came to Lublin. I met my former sweetheart there. Our meeting was a mira-cle, but when you don't have faith, you don't see the mira-cles. We had one answer for everything—chance. The world was chance, man was chance, and everything that happened to him was chance. In Warsaw I had been a member of the Young Men of Zion. My father, may he rest in peace, had a dry-goods store on Gesia Street and I helped him out a bit there and gave the rest of my time to Party affairs and reading.

My girlfriend, Celia, was an avowed Communist. We often waged fiery discussions. When I disagreed with her, she said what all Communists say in such instances—that after the revolution she'd hang me from the nearest lamppost. But in the meantime, we went to the opera and often to lectures at the Yiddish Writers' Club. You weren't lecturing at that time, but you did publish in the *Literary Pages.* Both Celia and I were devoted readers of this magazine, although I didn't like its leftist views and Celia felt it wasn't leftist enough. We liked Yiddish literature, Yiddish culture, and all the rest. We attended the Yiddish theater. Celia came from a Hasidic family, too. Her father was a follower of the Gur rabbi and her brothers wore long earlocks. They all perished.

When we met in Lublin again, it was almost like a resurrection of the dead. I had been sure she was dead and she considered me a corpse, too. She was already cured of the Communist affliction. Anyone who lives in that country can no longer nurse any illusions. But naturally we both remained what is called progressive. I remained a Zionist, and she still believed that socialism was the cure for all the world's ills. Certainly Stalin was no good, but if Trotsky or Kamenev had remained in power, or if the Bolsheviks and the Mensheviks had united, Russia would now be a paradise. *You* know their delusions: "If Grandmother had wheels, she'd be a trolley." At our very first reunion we discussed how to save the world, as befits two members of the intelligentsia. Soon we took our bundles and struck out in the direction of Germany. You couldn't do anything legally then—we had no passports or other papers. The worldly laws are so designed that if you don't want to be a partner to their crimes you must become a victim of their crimes. We have our own country now, thank God, but our leaders learned much from the Gentiles. Don't stand here and don't sit there. Everything is forbidden. They mock the Shulhan Arukh, but their codes of laws, excuse the comparison, has a thousand more restrictions than ours. But more of that later.

Of course, neither of us was a virgin any longer. What would have restrained us? Walking and dragging our packs and fearing murderers of every kind, we confessed to each other. While we starved in Russia, and—if you'll forgive me—deloused ourselves, we indulged in love affairs. I had Jewish women, young shiksas, and older Russian women, and she had her own adventures. The truth is that I had never forgotten her. Although I did not believe in the hereafter, I often spoke to her soul and justified myself for the way I was living. Celia told me that she had had similar feelings about me. Why drag it out? We got married in a German D.P. camp not far from Munich. I hoped to get a visa to Israel, but it just so happened that in 1947 we got visas to America. All the refugees envied us—what luck to go to the Golden Land!

We sailed to Halifax and from there took a train to the States. Celia had learned how to be a seamstress in Russia and a half dozen other trades. I had wandered as far as Tashkent. I had no trade, but my father had been a merchant, and when you're born into a business household, you've got business in your blood. I began by working in a dry-goods store in New York, but another refugee proposed that I become his partner in a bungalow that he was about to build. This was the beginning of our real estate business. The one bungalow became ten, the ten—fifty. I began to earn big money. Celia decided to continue her interrupted studies and enrolled in Hunter College. She had graduated from the Gymnasium in Warsaw and had dragged her diploma over all the borders. She had also been a student at the Wszechnica, a free university. She finished college in a few years with honors; in the meantime, I had become a wealthy man. We rented a big apartment on West End Avenue and had a summer home in Connecticut. But we had no children. Celia had had an operation and she could no longer get pregnant.

Now that I've become what I am, all these things seem foolish to me. What did I need with all that money? And what good did the education do Celia? She studied literature but the whole course consisted of taking some bad writer and ascribing meanings to him that he himself never even dreamed of. Well then, are the so-called good writers any good either? What important things did Eliot or Joyce have in mind when they were writing their empty phrases? What did they want? One page of *The Path of the Righteous* contains more wisdom and psychology than all their writings. They're often boring, too, because they have nothing to say. She often read me her literary essays. She had learned good English. But during all this time we still read the Yiddish newspapers, and we didn't miss a word you published. Whatever it may have been you said, at least you said it clearly. You know all the faults of modern man, no doubt, but you don't want to elaborate on the consequences of your knowledge. If you took one step farther, you'd become a full-fledged Jew.

"To know faults isn't enough," I interrupted.

"You also know all the good traits of the real Jew."

"That's not enough either. For this you must have faith that everything stated in the holy books was given to Moses on Mount Sinai. Unfortunately, I don't have this faith."

"Why do you say 'unfortunately'?"

"Because I envy those that do."

"We'll talk more about this. Faith doesn't come by itself. You must work for it." He went on with his story.

* * *

When a person makes a lot of money but lacks faith, he begins to concern himself with one thing: how to squeeze in all the pleasure possible. Often in the midst of all the hustling I'd ask myself, What do I gain from all this money? What does my material world consist of? I don't need to be a rich man to eat! The people with whom I associated, my partners and others, only kept boasting about their conquests of women. Woe to those conquests! They spent time with call girls, plain whores that a madam sent to the motel when they phoned her. Others had mistresses. In the circles in which we traveled, adultery was considered the highest virtue, the very essence of life. Literature was nothing but a textbook of lechery. The theater presented more adultery, and so did movies and television. These conquests aren't conquests at all, since modern women want the same as modern men. They read the same books, go to the same theaters, and have more free time than men.

The fact is that Celia satisfied me and I had no need of others, but she often expressed a kind of wonder that I wasn't having any outside affairs. When we went to the theater, the play often showed a wife deceiving her husband, and Celia laughed and applauded all the sly tricks and obscenities. In the theater, the father and wage earner is always presented as an idiot, and the lover is the wise one because he gets everything free. I often felt that there was something wrong in this attitude. Somehow I knew that Bolshevism, Hitlerism, and all the misfortunes of humanity stem from this contempt for the Ten Commandments. But how did you put it? "When you lack faith, what can you lean on?" At times I'd jokingly ask Celia, "Since you're so enamored of modern culture and so fond of modern plays, how is it you haven't taken a lover?" And she'd reply, "I'm too involved in my work." We kidded ourselves as modern couples do who, even when they aren't unfaithful, constantly tease each other and threaten infidelity.

After some time I let myself be swayed by my partners

and acquaintances to go sniffing around for whores. But the moment it came down to brass tacks, I'd be filled with such revulsion that I literally had to vomit. I didn't feel the slightest desire for them. The sex organs, for which wise guys have so many ugly names, express the soul of a man. They are by nature moral, spiritual, intended for love and devotion and reproduction. The Cabala calls the sex organs signs of the Holy Covenant. They are symbols of God's covenant with man, the image of God. I don't have to tell you this; you've studied and you know.

Well, since whores were repugnant to me, I had to find a so-called decent woman. That's how the expression goes—decent. What today's man considers a decent woman, our grandfathers considered a whore. They dress like whores, they talk like whores, they read filthy books, they only seek adventures. Their "decency" consists of the fact that they don't walk the streets looking for customers, and for this they demand a higher rate of pay. I found myself a woman like this. Her name was Liza. She had had a husband but she was divorced. She had a daughter in college who joined the hippies, although at that time they may not have been called that. What's the difference? Liza supposedly had a job, but she complained that it didn't pay enough to support both her and her daughter. She became my mistress and began to milk me for money. I paid her rent, took her to restaurants and theaters, bought her clothes, furniture, what not? But she needed more than I was willing to give her. Those who take from others never have enough. And just as she grabbed from me, her daughter grabbed from her. She wrote alarming letters from college and Liza showed them to me; a few times the girl came to New York. Knowing that I helped her mother out with money, she was particularly sweet to me, kissed me, hugged me, and told me that she regarded me as a father. Her mother even hinted that if I was good to her daughter, she would be good to me. I knew full well what she meant.

Already by then, even during moments of passion, I sensed the tawdriness of this affair. I had bought love just like my partners. Well, when a man marries he also supports his family. Didn't I provide Celia with all her needs? Hadn't my father supported my mother? It's true that my mother had a half dozen children with my father, ran the household, and worked even harder than he. But those were other times, other attitudes. Liza was often very passionate when she was with me, acted loving, and even tried to persuade me to divorce Celia and marry her. She told me her life story, all her problems and disappointments. According to her, she was a victim of male brutality. All she ever wanted was to be a faithful wife and a good mother, but she had married a charlatan, and so forth and so on. She had divorced him and he had promised to pay her alimony, but he moved to another state and didn't pay a penny. She had been forced to work and slave to raise her daughter.

I sometimes heard Liza trying to lecture her daughter, but the girl responded with insolence. The daughter was even more greedy than the mother. Once she was arrested with a group for smoking marijuana, and I had to put up bail to get her out. She studied sociology, the so-called science of how to make the world better. While they befouled the world, they became experts on how to save it. I wasn't so insensitive as not to see the shame and deception of all this, but I still wallowed in the slime because it offered me alleged comfort and because there was nowhere else to go—or so I told myself. What option did I have? To grow a beard and earlocks and become a pious Jew, like my father and grandfather? How did you put it earlier: "For that you must have faith," and I had no faith at all that Moses gave the Torah that he took from Heaven. I had read the Bible critics who guaranteed me that everything said in our holy books was false. Didn't the Mishnah make out of one law in the Pentateuch eighteen laws, and the Gemara, from the eighteen, seventy? Hadn't the rabbis added new restrictions in every generation?

Sometimes pious Jews with beards, earlocks, and hats just like this I'm wearing now came to my office asking for donations for yeshivas. I'd throw them a few dollars, but with resentment. I hated their sponging ways. I asked them, "Who needs so many yeshivas? And how did the yeshivas help when Hitler came to power? Where was God when they burned His Torah and ordered those who studied it to dig their own graves?" The Jews had no answers to this, or so it seemed then. The fact is that when they tried to talk to me, I interrupted and told them I had no time. I was sure beforehand that they couldn't supply the answers to my questions. I gave them handouts convinced that it was money thrown away.

I needn't tell you that people milked money from me on all sides. I often gave to causes in which I hadn't the slightest interest and to people whom I didn't trust at all. The pious Jews demanded that I support the Torah and the secular ones begged for culture. Culture here, culture there. I often felt like asking, "What is this culture of yours? Where does it lead? What kind of people will it raise?" The yeshivas, I felt, would raise daydreamers and parasites. Well, and whom and what would the culture raise? I knew it even then: cynics and whores. But I didn't dare say anything, for what was I myself but a whoremonger? I wallowed deep in the mud, convinced at the same time that one cannot crawl out of it. If yeshivas were no good, perhaps the theater was. If both were no good, then *what* was worthwhile?. . .

Celia noticed that I was busier than I used to be, for I would often come home late. Although I had told Liza not to phone me at home, she did so anyhow. Celia began to tease me that I had a sweetheart. Since I was afraid that she'd make a scandal or revenge herself by taking a lover, I flatly denied it. I thought up all kinds of excuses. I took false oaths, too. Liza's demands kept growing. She gave up her job. She needed a bigger apartment, since the daughter would be coming to live with her now. No matter how much I gave her, she lamented that it wasn't enough. The daughter arrived, bringing along her lover. He had red hair and the face of a murderer. He said almost the same things Celia used to say when she was a Communist: that the revolution would soon erupt and I would be promptly liquidated. The masses, he claimed, were losing patience. I said to him, "Is it my fault I was born into a capitalist system? Can a man pick out his system?" But he said, "When the masses grow tired of bearing the burden, they don't want to know about guilt or innocence. They kill, burn, and do whatever they want. That's revolution."

"Yes, that's revolution," agreed Liza's daughter, the student of sociology.

I told them they had no guarantee that the same mobs wouldn't liquidate them, too. I told them that many Jewish Reds who had threatened me and my kind with the gallows had themselves died in Soviet prisons or been tortured in Stalin's slave camps. But this sounded to them like some fairy tale. Here in America things would be different. Here the masses would know exactly who was a friend and who an enemy. Even if they made a mistake, it would be no misfortune. Errors were made in all revolutions . . .

Liza's daughter lived with that brute literally before her mother's eyes. They were constantly kissing and fondling each other. They spoke with the highest regard about all kinds of terrorists. The mother tried to contradict them, especially when I was present, but they made mincemeat of her. What did she know about such things? They were always carrying books, pamphlets, appeals, petitions. The telephone kept ringing. Liza now had a separate room that she had designated as "my," Joseph Shapiro's, room. When it grew too painful for me to argue with the daughter and the "son-in-law" (as I called him), Liza took me into "my" room and all she talked about was how expensive everything was becoming and how hard it was for her to meet her obligations. I was not only supporting Liza but her daughter and the man who promised me death when the masses arose, but I seldom dared to say something to Liza about her precious child. She would promptly bawl and grow hysterical. What did I have against Micki (that was the daughter's pet name)? She was still a child. She had grown up without a father, poor thing. Naturally, Liza would have preferred that Micki marry a doctor, a lawyer, even a dentist, rather than run around with this roughneck from Texas—but who could give today's children advice? It was another world, a different time.

Yes, it was another world and a different time, but I lay deep in the mire and did the Devil's work.

And now comes the episode that changed my life.

2

It was a cold winter day. I had spent the whole day with my partners on Long Island, where we were building. I phoned Celia to tell her that I wouldn't be home that night. She asked me the name of my hotel and I told her that I didn't know it yet since we had to go to a few other places and I wasn't sure where I'd be sleeping. Our telephone conversations, as our other talks generally, were curt. Actually, I had arranged with Liza to have supper at her house and spend the night with her. Liza prided herself on being a good cook. She said to me more than once that the best way to a man's heart was through his stomach. I'm not much of an eater, but she cooked the kinds of dishes I remembered from home and I often complimented her on them.

I finished my work as quickly as possible, and exactly at six I knocked on her door. I was afraid that I'd find her daughter and her lover there, but thank God they were out of town. That evening Liza's apartment seemed more attractive and comfortable than usual. It was freezing cold outside but inside. it was nice and warm. She had lots of time, and she polished and cleaned the furniture, the rugs, and the silver so that every corner of the apartment sparkled. The smell of my favorite dishes drifted in from the kitchen. Liza and I had cocktails, then sat down to eat. Between one course and the next, she bewailed her fate. She was alone. Her daughter was giving her trouble, pressing her for money, because her lover had forgotten to be careful and had impregnated her. Micki needed an abortion and this cost no less than seven hundred dollars for a good doctor who wouldn't endanger her life. The lover didn't have a penny and Micki had come whining to her mother. These words repelled me so that the food stuck in my gullet. I was supposed to pay for the abandon of some wild youth with the eyes and face of a killer. I said that if Micki was ripe enough to live with a man, she should have enough sense to be careful. Liza began to weep bitter tears. What could she do? That was the younger generation. If she said a wrong word to Micki, the girl promptly threatened to kill herself, or convert, or do whatever came to her mind.

Liza cried and cried until I couldn't stand it and I promised to give her the seven hundred dollars. This besides the other moneys that she wheedled out of me under various pretexts.

This ruined not only our supper but our sex as well. When a man gets angry and feels exploited and humiliated, he loses his passion. I tried to restore my potency with whiskey, but it didn't help. I lay impotent next to Liza, feeling as if old age had settled upon me. She tried to arouse me with good words, with false words, with sharp words, and even with smut, but nothing helped. Finally she accused me of not loving her. I wanted to ask, "Why should I love you? What is there about you to love? Love must go with respect, but how can I respect a woman who milks me of money, not only for herself, but for two young and healthy brutes, neither of whom intend to do some decent work?" I thought of my parents, of my grandparents, and I felt as if I had betrayed them and the whole of Jewish history. I remembered what I had heard and read about our martyrs in Poland; how Jews had donned prayer shawls and phylacteries and gone off to the cemeteries to die martyrs' deaths. I was descended from such Jews, I had been taught their Torah, but what had I traded it all for?

I fell asleep, but instead of bringing me comfort, sleep only intensified my pain. I dreamed that I was in a cellar with my parents and other Jews hiding from the Nazis. Shooting, wild screams could be heard outside. Suddenly someone lit a match and in the flash of light I saw that I was dressed as a Nazi in a brown uniform and a swastika. A fear came over me. How could this be? And what would the Jews say if someone lit another match and they saw who was among them? In the dream I felt that my Nazi uniform was the result of my way of life. More than anything I feared the disgrace that I would cause my parents. I awoke from the nightmare exhausted.

Suddenly there was a loud, insistent ring at the front door. Liza had dozed off, too, but she awoke with a start. "Who can that be?" she asked. "I won't open." But the ringing grew ever more insistent. Liza slipped on a robe and went to the door. As I lay there, I heard muttering and angry whispers. I realized at once that it was Micki. The mother and daughter began arguing, and soon the whispers became shouts. It didn't take long before I heard screams and the sound of blows. Micki was beating her mother. I threw on a robe and ran to separate them. I came in to see Micki holding her mother's hair and dealing her blow after blow.

Liza was screaming, "Whore! Bitch! Tramp!"

And Micki responded with, "And what are you? I know all your tricks. You change men like gloves. It was you who made me what I am. You have two lovers now!" Micki hit her so hard I was afraid that she'd kill her.

"Liar! Thief! Prostitute! Out of my house!" Liza screamed in a wild voice.

"Yes, you have two lovers and you suck money from them both!"

And Micki told all the details of her mother's conduct, naming names. Liza fell on the floor and began to gasp spasmodically.

The daughter cried, "That's the last time I'll ever look at you, you old strumpet!"

I began to dress quickly. I wanted to vomit. I was afraid that the fight between mother and daughter would end in murder. I recalled what I had learned as a boy: if you broke one of the Ten Commandments, you would break them all. I dressed hurriedly.

Liza lay on the floor like a bundle of rags. Suddenly she leaped up and began to shriek, "She's a liar! A liar! Don't go! Where are you going? Oh, I'll kill her!. . ."

She ran into the kitchen and came back with a knife. Her eyes were wild, her face drained, her mouth twisted. The daughter tried to take the knife away from her. I managed to reach the door and raced down the stairs because the elevator wasn't fast enough. I ran down so many stairs that it seemed as if the house had a hundred floors. When I tried to exit from the staircase into the lobby, it turned out that the door was locked. My heart was pounding and I was dizzy. I went down into the cellar, where the oil tanks and the gas meters were located, and a drunken man began to shout at me and wave his fists. I managed somehow to explain my predicament and gave him a dollar. He led me to the lobby, and from there I went out into the street and looked for a cab. The frost cut like a knife, and the wind tore at my hat and slapped my face. I felt frozen, and there wasn't a taxi in sight. All of a sudden one appeared, and I started to wave my arms. I was half frozen and my spiritual bitterness forced a physical bitterness up from my stomach into my mouth. I again felt like throwing up and I had to make a superhuman effort not to befoul the cab. As usual when in trouble, I forgot my heresy and begged God to spare me this humiliation, too. I could have told the driver to stop and gotten out to vomit, but he looked like an angry man. He didn't say a word to me, only grunted to himself. His face reflected the rage of those who stay up nights. Somehow I managed to control myself. When we reached my house I handed the driver a ten-dollar bill. He made a gesture to give me change, but I couldn't wait any longer and I motioned him to go. All the time I was sitting in the cab, I was afraid that he might rob me or even kill me. He looked to me like a criminal.

As soon as the cab had gone, I stooped over a pile of snow and vomited up all the good food and drinks that Liza had served me. I soiled my coat. My whole being was one skein of bitterness, sourness, and shame over my own degradation. There was supposed to be a doorman in the lobby, but I knew very well where he was—down in the basement playing cards with the cop whose duty it was to patrol the street and protect the inhabitants. You couldn't say a word about this because, for all the fine talk about democracy, law, and freedom, the world always did and still does follow the principle of might makes right. Now that Jews mimic Gentiles, they follow the same principle. Even in those days someone was being killed in New York every other day and the police never found the perpetrator. If he was found, the lawyers promptly bailed him out and the court later freed him for lack of evidence. If a witness did show up, he had to be kept in confinement to protect him from the criminals. In America, as in Sodom, the perpetrator went free and the witness rotted in jail. And all this was done in the name of liberalism. The whole worldly justice protects the criminal and leaves the actual or potential victim at his mercy. Everyone knows this, but try talking about it and you're called the worst names. In my own business you had to constantly hand out bribes to inspectors, police, all kinds of officials.

The mayor knew this. It was, as they say, an open secret. Today's Jew is no better than the Gentile. He often exploits this situation for his own ends and for profits. Many lawyers teach the criminals how to circumvent the law, to make a mockery of it, and I myself was part of this system.

3

After I recovered, I rode the elevator to my floor. I had broken up with Liza for good, and I thought, So many people are satisfied with one wife, why can't I be, too? In comparison to Liza, Celia now seemed decency itself. She had studied and was trying to find a job, a profession. I had an excuse ready for Celia as to why I had come home in the middle of the night. A man who lives with several women becomes an expert at telling lies. I was fool enough to think that Celia believed my lies. It's a rule that those who deceive others also deceive themselves. Every liar is convinced that he can fool the whole world. Actually, *he* is fooled more than anyone else.

I had a key to my apartment, but the front door was bolted and chained from inside. I rang the doorbell, but Celia didn't answer. I rang again and again, ever more firmly and insistently. I kept on ringing. Celia had apparently sunk into a deep sleep and I would have to wake her, although she was normally a light sleeper. I began to fear that some tragedy had befallen her. Our apartment had two entrances, a front and a rear. I had a key to the back door. A door led to a corridor running from the passenger elevator to the freight elevator where the garbage was put out. I opened this door and saw the back door to my apartment open and a man come out. I knew him—he was one of the professors supervising Celia's thesis. Behind him stood Celia in her nightgown. My dear friend, there occurred in my house that which is shown in all the melodramas and cheap films: the husband coming unexpectedly home and the wife sneaking her lover out the back door. I grew so ashamed that I closed the door again. Maimonides says somewhere that Gehenna is shame. In that moment, I experienced the shame that is Gehenna.

In the melodramas, the husband assaults the lover and they fight to the death, but I was in no mood to wage combat against this elderly lecher. I waited until I could no longer hear his footsteps on the stairs, and in the meantime, Celia opened the front door for me. Then she ran and locked herself in the bathroom. That night, I drained the cup of misery to its very dregs, as the phrase goes, and I knew what I must do: put an end to the kind of life I'd been leading, sever for once and all my ties with everything and everybody in my environment. I had been dealt a blow that I could not ignore. Actually, I had known right along that my life was a shame and a disgrace—all that chasing after money, my affairs with women, being part of a society that was corrupt from beginning to end and whose justice was the encouragement of crime.

Celia took her time in the bathroom, which gave me the opportunity to collect my things and to pack the most necessary ones. Fortunately, I found a passport that was valid for a few more years. I also had a bankbook and a number of important documents that I kept at home. I heard Celia coughing in the bathroom. From time to time, the water ran as if she was washing. The whole packing took me some three-quarters of an hour. I was afraid that Celia would rush out and start all the talk and justifications that are employed in such situations, but she was silent. I had the feeling that she guessed I was packing my things and had decided to wait until I was gone.

I took my two satchels and left. I walked down the stairs and was soon out in the cold street again. I knew that not only was I leaving my house but I was beginning a new life. I couldn't remain out in the street. The frost was biting and an icy wind blew. A taxi came by and I told the driver to take me to the first hotel I could think of. I signed the register with the first name that came to my mind. I had lost my wife, my mistress, and my business as well, because I no longer wished to remain in New York or even in America—but I felt no sense of loss. I lay down in bed and slept the sleep of total resignation. When I opened my eyes the sun was shining. I decided to turn everything I owned into cash, and whatever couldn't be quickly liquidated, I would simply abandon. I wouldn't say that I felt reborn; it was more the feeling of one who has just died and whose soul has entered a strange body.

My first impulse was to take a bath or shower, and go down to the restaurant or coffee shop for breakfast. I even considered ordering eggs with ham or bacon. But I quickly reminded myself that last night in the cab I had decided to be a Jew, and a Jew didn't eat pork. At the same time I knew how fraught with problems my decision would be. To be a Jew, to adhere to the laws of the Shulhan Arukh, one had to—as you said before—believe in the Torah and the Gemara, and that everything that all the rabbis wrote was given by Moses on Mount Sinai. But I didn't have this faith. I had read much, first in Warsaw, later in Russia, and later still in America, and somehow it wasn't easy for me to accept the notion that along with the Ten Commandments Moses had received all the interpretations and all the restrictions of the rabbis of all generations. I hated the modern world and everything it represented—its barbarism, its licentiousness, its false justice, its wars, its Hitlers, its Stalins, everything—but I had no proof whatsoever that the Torah had been given by God or that there even was a God. True, there had to be some force that moved the universe, I told myself. I had never been a materialist who contends that the universe was created by an explosion and that everything evolved on its own. I had read a history of philosophy, and although I'm no philosopher, I saw how foolish, how weak and unconvincing all their theories were. Actually, all modern philosophy has a single theme: we don't know anything and we cannot know anything. Our small brain isn't capable of grasping eternity, infinity, or even the essence of the things which we see and touch. But to what did this lead? Their ethics weren't worth a fig and committed no one to anything. You could be versed in all their philosophies and still be a Nazi or a member of the KGB. I hadn't been only physically stripped that day, but spiritually bared as well.

Such was my mood that morning when I went down to the restaurant for breakfast. I bought a newspaper, and as I turned the pages I found everything there that I wanted to escape from: wars, glorification of revolution, murders, rapes, politicians' cynical promises, lying editorials, acclaim of stupid books, dirty plays and films. The paper paid tribute to every possible kind of idolatry and spat at truth. According to the editors, if the voters would only choose the President they recommended, and put into effect this or the other reform, all would be right with the world. Even the obituary page was made to seem somehow optimistic. It listed all the accomplishments of those who died, and displayed their photographs. A theatrical producer had died and the account enumerated all the trashy plays he had produced, all the smut he had presented on stage. The fact that he had died relatively young was glossed over. The emphasis was on the fact that he had accumulated a big estate, which he left to his fourth or fifth wife.

That day a murderer was arrested, one who had been charged with the same crime several times before but each time had been freed on bail or paroled. His photograph was printed, too, along with the name of his lawyer, whose function it was to teach this murderer how to avoid punishment so that he could kill more innocent people.

Yes, there was much to escape from and to reject. But escape to where? There was religious news in the paper too. It told of two Christian organizations that were merging like two firms on Wall Street, and of some rabbi who was getting a medal. He stood there among ladies who smiled sweetly at him for the camera while he smiled back and displayed the medal. He looked vulgar, and although supposedly a Jew, he had the most Gentile name that an assimilated Jew could pick out.

But what would *my* religion be? What could I believe in?. . .

The waitress came and I ordered breakfast. I watched someone at the next table working away at his plate of ham with eggs. I had long since come to the conclusion that man's treatment of God's creatures makes mockery of all his ideals and of the whole alleged humanism. In order for this overstuffed individual to enjoy his ham, a living creature had to be raised, dragged to its death, stabbed, tortured, scalded in hot water. The man didn't give a second's thought to the fact that the pig was made of the same stuff as he and that it had to pay with suffering and death so that he could taste its flesh. I've thought more than once that when it comes to animals, every man is a Nazi. I had pondered this often, but somehow I had never come to any resolution. I myself bought a fur coat for Liza made from the skins of dozens of creatures. With what rapture and enthusiasm she

27

stroked the fur of those butchered animals. How she poured out praises for skins torn from the bodies of others!

Yes, I had always felt these things, but that morning they literally hit me on the head like a hammer. That morning I realized for the first time what a horrible hypocrite I was.

4

The first decision I made had no direct bearing on religion,
but to me it represented a religious decision. To wit: to eat
no more meat or fish, nothing that had ever lived and been
killed for food. Even when I was a businessman who wanted
to become rich, even as I deceived others and myself, too, I
knew that I was living against my convictions and that my
way of life was false and corrupt. I was myself a liar, but I
hated lies and deceit of every kind. I was a lecher, but I felt a
revulsion against loose women and against wantonness in
general. I ate meat, but a shudder ran through me each time I
reminded myself how meat becomes meat. I've studied
enough to know that the Torah regards the eating of flesh as
a "necessary evil." The Torah speaks with contempt of
those who yearn for the fleshpots of meat. I had always felt
the greatest sympathy for those groups in India who practice
vegetarianism as part of their religion. Everything that had
to do with slaughtering, skinning, and hunting always
evoked disgust within me and guilt feelings that words can-

not describe. I sometimes thought that even if a voice from Heaven decreed the slaughter of animals and the shedding of their blood to be a virtue, I would respond like that Tanna who said, "We don't care about voices from Heaven." As you can see, I've turned back to Jewishness, but even among the pious I live with, I've remained a kind of misfit. They often reproach me, "You needn't be more saintly than the saints. You must not pity creatures more than the Almighty does." Some reprove me for not eating meat or fish on the Sabbath. But I always tell them, "If I'm fated to end up in Gehenna for not eating meat, I take this punishment upon myself gladly. I am absolutely convinced that so long as people shed the blood of God's creatures, there'll be no peace on earth. It's one step from spilling animal blood to spilling human blood." For me, thou shalt not kill includes animals, too. I managed to persuade my present wife to my way of thinking. We are a family of vegetarians.

It would take too long to describe to you everything that I went through since the day I lost my wife, my mistress, and my business. One minute I was bound to mundane society with a thousand threads, or chains, and the next I was cut off from everything and everybody. The first thing I did that morning was to turn everything I had into traveler's checks. The bank tellers wondered why I was buying them in such large amounts. They asked where I was headed and I told them I was going on a round-the-world trip, with stops in many countries. They all said the same thing—that they envied me. One girl asked me if my wife was going along, and I told her I was a widower. In a sense, this wasn't a lie. I felt that my whole world had died.

I constantly told myself that only one way out remained for me: to return to Jewishness, and not merely to some modern arbitrary Jewishness, but to the Jewishness of my grandfathers and great-grandfathers. But there arose the question of all questions: Did I also possess their faith? And I answered myself clearly and sincerely, No, I did not possess their faith. "In that case, what sense does it make to return to the Jewishness of your grandfathers?" a voice within me asked. "You won't be a real Jew, you'll merely be playing the part. You'll be like those actors who put on prayer shawls and portray saints and rabbis on stage, then go home and revert to their rotten ways." The same voice went on: "Don't make a fool of yourself and ruin your life. You're an unbeliever like all other unbelievers, and you must live their life. If your wife has been unfaithful to you, find one that will be true or get a mistress who will suit your needs. To throw yourself into Jewishness without believing that every word in the Shulhan Arukh is sacred is what is called in Yiddish laying a healthy head on a sick pillow. You'll be something neither here nor there, a paradox, a hypocrite."

But another voice interjected: "All other ways except extreme Jewishness must lead to the lies and lewdness you despise. If you don't believe in the Shulhan Arukh, then you must believe in evil and in all kinds of empty and bankrupt theories that lead to the abyss. When a man is drowning and sees a life preserver, he doesn't ask who threw it, how long it might last, or other such questions. A drowning man even clutches at a straw. You saw with your own eyes what licentiousness leads to: The KGB, the Gestapo. If you don't want to be a Nazi, you must become the opposite. It's no accident that Hitler and his theoreticians waged such a savage war against the *Talmud Jude*. These villains rightfully sensed that the Talmud and the Talmud Jew were their greatest enemy. A Jew without God can easily be persuaded that Lenin, Trotsky, or Stalin will bring deliverance. Jews without God can believe that Karl Marx was the Messiah. Jews without faith not only clutch at straws but even at burned straws. Every few months they find a new idol, a new illusion, a new vogue, a new madness. They revere all kinds of murderers, whores, false prophets, clowns. They go wild over every little scribbler, every ham actor, every harlot.

Even if Moses' Torah and the Talmud are nothing more than the works of men, they are still the mightiest barrier against wickedness. The Talmud Jew doesn't kill. He doesn't take part in wild orgies. You don't have to fear him in the woods or on a lonely road. He doesn't carry a gun. He doesn't scheme to come to your house when you are away and sleep with your wife. He has no wish to dishonor your daughter. Although he didn't adopt Christianity, he's been turning his other cheek for two thousand years, while those who profess Christian love often plucked out his beard, along with a piece of the cheek. This Talmud Jew doesn't deal violently with any race, class, or group. All he wants is to earn a living and raise his children and children's children to follow in the ways of the Torah and the Shulhan Arukh. He wants to raise chaste daughters instead of whores. He doesn't need modern literature, theater, nude art. He doesn't change his outlook every Monday and Thursday.

"It's true that not all Talmud Jews are saints. There are degrees among them, too. There are those who act unethically, chase after honors, and become involved in all kinds of Hasidic cliques and quarrels. But even the worst among them don't murder, don't hunt, don't rape, don't justify killing, don't scheme to liquidate whole classes and races, don't transform family life into a joke. Besides, why take an example from the worst rather than from the best? There is trash everywhere. Actually, if a man is a swindler, he's not a Jew anymore."

That's what the other voice said, and this was a mighty voice and I knew that morning that it would never be silenced again. In a moment, it cried out to me: "If one idolatry demands blood and shame and the other idolatry demands compassion and purity, then serve the latter."

I recalled those Jewish Communists who called Chmielnitzky a liberator of the masses. I also thought of the Jewish revolutionaries in the second half of the nineteenth century who justified the pogroms in Russia as an expression of the people's rebellion against the tsar. And what about the praises that their counterparts in our generation sang to Stalin, knowing he had murdered and tortured millions of innocent people, including hundreds of thousands of Jews, and all in the name of the holy revolution, which is the Baal and the Moloch of many modern Jews? There wasn't an evil these Red Jews wouldn't justify if they felt it greased the wheels of what they called progress.

"What concrete steps can I take now?" I asked the voice, and it replied: "Go to a house of prayer and pray."

"Without faith?" I countered, and the voice said: "You have more faith than you know."

I knew of no synagogues or houses of prayer in the neighborhood in which I now found myself. I had no prayer shawl or phylacteries. The whole idea of praying seemed wild to me, but the voice wouldn't let up. It offered me practical advice: "Take a cab downtown to East Broadway and the streets thereabouts. There you will find what you are seeking. If you want to be a Jew, you must begin right now."

I hailed a cab and told the driver to take me to the Lower East Side. I sat in the cab astounded and ashamed at what was happening to me. The other voice mocked me: "So you're becoming pious because a couple of females gave you horns? Your piety is a lie and a self-deception. This God to whom you're going to pray doesn't exist. Where was He when the Jews of Poland dug their own graves? Where was He when the Nazis played with the skulls of Jewish children? If He does exist and He kept silent, He is as much a murderer as Hitler."

With such thoughts and feelings I arrived where I had asked to be driven. For many minutes I walked around without finding a house of prayer. I came to a small synagogue but they had finished praying and the doors were locked. I was already planning to put off my newly awakened Jewishness till tomorrow. The Almighty had waited so long, the scoffer within me noted, He would wait another day. Suddenly something happened which at that moment I considered a miracle. A Jew with a gray beard stopped me and said, "Maybe you'd like to join a minyan? Come inside. We need one more." And the man mentioned the name of some rabbi who was waiting for a tenth Jew.

I stood there dumbfounded.

"I was actually looking for a house of prayer," I said.

"Come along, then."

"But I don't have a prayer shawl or phylacteries."

"We'll give you a prayer shawl and phylacteries."

I believed then and I still do that this was no coincidence. The powers that watch over every human being, every insect and worm, had directed me onto the path I was destined to tread and which I chose after many tribulations. I let myself be escorted by the man. We came to an old building and walked up a stoop to the apartment where they were waiting for me.

5

The house where the rabbi lived was of the type condemned to be razed. I entered a narrow, dark hallway. The door opened and I came into a kind of American Hasidic study house that contained a holy ark, shelves of old books, a lectern, and benches. I might have been back in Warsaw, but the few men who were pacing around here wore not the cloth caps of Warsaw but crushed and spotted fedoras. They looked old, wrinkled, neglected. Their faces showed no trace of the fervor you'd find in a Warsaw Hasidic *shtibl*.

They gazed at me with bewilderment. Apparently I didn't look like the kind of man who would let himself be dragged to a minyan in the middle of the day.

One of them said, "I'll get the rabbi."

He vanished for a time, then came back with an old man with a white beard and a skullcap. He wore a faded coat that was unbuttoned to show a large ritual garment with fringes hanging nearly to the ankles. The rabbi was the size of a six-year-old boy. He had a sickly, swollen abdomen. His complexion was yellowish. I'm no doctor, but when I looked at him I knew that he was deathly ill. He didn't walk but shuffled his feet. His eyes reflected a softness I had already forgotten in America. This was a person who couldn't hurt a fly. I realized that his swelling came from illness, not overeating. I greeted him and his voice was as mild as his gaze.

He extended a soft hand to me and asked, "Where are you from?"

"I'm from Poland, but I've been in America for several years."

"Where were you during the Holocaust?"

I told him and found out that he had been in Maidenek. This was the first time I had met a pious Jew who had been saved from the Nazi villains. I asked him which rabbinical court he came from and he named one that wasn't familiar to me.

In a short while, we gathered to pray. I had grown accustomed to the rapid pace at which Americans do everything, but here they moved along with unusual slowness. It took a good half hour for the old man to put on his prayer shawl and phylacteries. I looked at his old prayer shawl and I knew that soon it and the old body under it would be lying in the grave. Someone had already told me that the rabbi suffered from bad kidneys and that he retained water. I watched as he wound the thongs around his arm and mumbled. How such a body could survive Maidenek, I'll never understand.

I stood gazing at a martyr, one of those saints who are supposed to carry the world on their shoulders. With what fervor he recited the blessings! He had to strain to put on the phylacteries, even to kiss the fringes. I could see that each move meant agony. The soul just barely reposed in this saintly body. I couldn't bring myself to believe that I had been so privileged as to see this remnant of old Jewishness with my own eyes. One of the men suggested that the rabbi sit down for the Eighteen Benedictions, but he wouldn't hear of it.

I saw how he slowly raised a trembling hand and smote his breast as he uttered: "We have sinned" and "We have transgressed." He, the saint, repented his uncommitted sins while millions of evildoers boasted of murder and tens of thousands of lawyers—Jews among them—sought means of freeing every thief, robber, swindler, and rapist. I was seized by a sense of self-shame. There were saints in New York but I had spent my time with whores, with sly exploiters, with manufacturers who dallied with call girls. Now I had a prayer shawl and phylacteries that someone had lent me but I had forgotten how to wind the thongs so that they formed the letter *shin* of the word *shaddai*—God.

I prayed and saw to my amazement that this was far from comedy and sham. I thanked the Creator for directing me to this room among true Jews, who still sought a minyan while the outside world swarmed with hate and evil theories. Here, old age was no disgrace. Here, no one boasted of his sexual prowess or his ability to hold liquor. Here, the elderly were treated with respect and pious humility. No one here dyed his hair, claimed to be "eighty years young," or used the other banalities heard among the worldly aged.

Up to that day I had been a reader of books, magazines, and newspapers. I had often felt that what I was reading was a deadly poison. All it evoked within me was bitterness, fear, and a feeling of helplessness. Everything that I read followed the same theme—the world was and will always be ruled by might and falsehood, and there was nothing to be done about it. Modern literature used different words to say the same thing: "We live in a slaughterhouse and a house of shame. That's how it was and that's how it's going to be forever." Suddenly I heard myself reciting words filled with holy optimism. Instead of starting the day with tales of theft and murder, lust and rape, obscenity and revenge, I had started the day with words about justice, sanctity, a God who had granted men understanding and who will revive the dead and reward the just. I had discovered that I didn't have to start the day by swallowing venom.

After praying, I did something which may appear to you melodramatic, but I'm not a literary man and I don't care whether I am dramatic or melodramatic. I announced to one and all: "I have money and whoever needs help can get it from me." I assumed that a commotion would erupt around me; that hands would stretch out and everyone would shout: "Give! Give!" as I was conditioned to expect among today's people who, no matter how much they took from you, were never satisfied. But these Jews only looked at me bewildered, and smiled as if I was playing a role for them. Only two of them told me that they were in need. I had a walletful of cash and I gave them as much as they needed. They seemed embarrassed, hesitated, and explained the reasons for their requests. The others said that they didn't need anything, but they all agreed that the truly needy one was the rabbi.

But when I asked the old man what I could do for him, he smiled a toothless smile and said, "I have everything I need, God be praised."

"Are you watching your health?"

"The doctors want me to go to the hospital, but I don't want to."

I knew his reasons. He didn't trust them to serve kosher food.

He said, "I'll live as long as I'm destined to live."

"Rabbi, I can get you a private room in a hospital and good doctors. They'll watch over you and—"

The rabbi's only response was, "*Et,*" meaning, I am not so sure . . . I can do without it . . . This is not our way of doing things . . . I have my doubts about it . . . and many similar such expressions of religious skepticism about worldly promises and means of imminent succor.

This *et* meant to say that it didn't pay to go to all that trouble.

The rebbetzin came in, a woman the rabbi's age, bent and wrinkled like old women used to be in my time, and wearing a bonnet.

I told her what I proposed to do for her husband and she said, "In the hospitals they'll start in with the tests, and those tests will kill him altogether."

She knew what she was talking about. I had already heard from other sick people that when certain doctors get hold of a patient he becomes a guinea pig on which they experiment. They draw blood from him and subject him to all kinds of suffering. Often these tests do more harm than the illness itself. The rebbetzin was the rabbi's second wife. The first had perished along with their children in Europe.

The rabbi began to tell me what he had suffered under the Nazis. His beard had been shorn. He had been made to dig graves and do other heavy labor. He had been beaten, too. He had said his confession each day, ready to die, but somehow the soul had refused to leave the body. I asked him whether he was connected with the orthodox organization in America and he again said, "*Et . . .*"

No, this wasn't the kind of rabbi the modern orthodox in America could send to conferences, have his picture taken, and let him raise funds at banquets where big budgets were being prepared. This was an old-fashioned Jew who needed nothing besides a glass of tea, some oat groats, a few old books, and a minyan. He had no urge to provide piety to the world or even to the community of Israel. He read no newspapers. He didn't know the kind of Yiddish that the modern orthodoxy had taken over from the unbelievers. He spoke like my grandfather and like your grandfather. The few Jews who supported him were just like him. Jewishness was to them a private thing, something between them and the Almighty.

I promised the rabbi that I'd come back in the evening and he nodded and thanked me. It was very hard to assemble a minyan.

I gave the rebbetzin a few dollars and she took them hesitantly and wished me many blessings. All America, all the Gentile and Jewish organizations kept yelling, "Give, give, give!" They put up buildings, hired more and more employees, banged away on typewriters, sought publicity. They all had one goal—success—whether they built a theater or a yeshiva, a university or a Torah Center, a summer camp or a ritual bath. But this heir to old Jewishness knew that money could not save or fortify Jewishness. The saints and *geonim* had come out of old study houses, yeshivas from which they went forth to different homes for their daily meals. Magnificent buildings, efficient secretaries, ringing telephones, and aggressive fund-raisers could produce only what they themselves represented: tumult and superficiality.

6

After I left the rabbi's house and walked the downtown streets, I got the feeling that it would be best if I remained somewhere close by, found a room or a small apartment in the neighborhood. I could pray three times a day with the minyan, and there was a vegetarian restaurant on Delancey Street. I walked past stores selling prayer books, prayer shawls, phylacteries, ritual garments, mezuzahs. Since the so-called new Jewishness was actually the same as worldliness—that is to say, full of falsehood, greed, and vanity—I had to return to the old Jewishness, which was newer than the newest of the new. I went into a store and picked out two holy books that happened to catch my eye: *The Path of the Righteous* by Moshe Haim Luzzatto and *The Voice of Elijah, a Commentary on Proverbs* by the Vilna Gaon. Afterward I went to the restaurant on Delancey Street and ordered a vegetarian meal. Enough slaughter of innocent creatures, enough gorging on the flesh and blood of others! The waiter brought me rolls and a plate of groats, beans, and mushrooms, all delicious. Why eat meat when there were such tasty dishes around?

As I ate, I glanced through the books. Whatever page I turned to, I encountered wisdom, not the ''wisdom'' dispensed by psychoanalysts, with their wild, unfounded theories and farfetched conclusions. The sum total of their teachings always was that someone else was guilty. The father had been too strict or the mother too despotic. They seized hold of a dream and probed it for all the answers to the patient's problems. Every page they wrote was full of not only contradictions but stupidity. The holy books, on the other hand, exuded a knowledge of mankind. Every word was precisely to the point. When I considered that the Freudians were deemed wise and innovative and these holy books obsolete, I had to laugh. How perverse modern man is! All he wants is to violate nature, and when it resists, he runs to psychiatrists for help.

Well, but what next? Where would I go from here? I asked myself.

Until now, the Evil One had been silent for some time, but now it got its voice back.

''Go home!'' it commanded. ''It's *your* apartment, *your* furniture. If you want to rid yourself of Celia, get a lawyer. No judge can force a husband to live with a wife he hates. In the worst instance, you'll pay her alimony for a couple of years. Call your partners. There's no reason in the world why you should leave them your business and become a homeless wanderer. If you want to be a pious Jew, you can do this in your own home. You don't have to leave America. There's no lack of synagogues, holy books, or rabbis here. The rabbi in whose house you prayed is a dying man and there are no more like him. That which Moshe Haim Luzzatto and the Vilna Gaon say may be all good and wise, but when a Hitler or a Stalin comes along, he squashes the Jews into dust and no one stands up for them. If you didn't have a pocketful of money right now, you'd have to stand out in the cold and beg.''

The Evil Spirit, or the beast within me, argued further: ''No, there are no more faithful wives, nor are there faithful husbands either. And you must come to terms with the notion that sex must be shared. There's no such thing anymore as sexual private property. In a sense, it's better this way. Faithfulness caused husbands and wives to grow tired of each other. It's like constantly eating the same dish. There'll come a time when every man will have dozens of women and every woman dozens of men. Each side will gain a lot of experience, and every meeting between husband and wife will become more interesting, piquant, and novel. Jealousy isn't an instinct but something you acquire. You can liberate yourself from it, and it opens up countless new perspectives, new experiences and satisfactions.''

The Devil remarked: ''I'd bet that Celia is searching for you right now, and phoning, and that she misses you. The fact that she slept with that old professor was nothing more than a whim, maybe a wish to revenge herself for your affairs, or a result of boredom. She'll be more interesting tonight. She'll embrace you in a different way, she'll show you new ways of love . . . As for Liza, you needn't take that so hard either. She's alone and she looks forward to your visits. She is a passionate woman. Since people need different foods, new clothes, new plays, and new books, why shouldn't they want new experiences in the most important areas of all, love and sex? You, Joseph Shapiro, won't make the world over. If that's the way things are everywhere, it's only a sign that this is the course of man's history, or God's plan.''

That's how the Devil within me moralized, and the words sounded so persuasive at that time that I was ready to grab a cab home. I longed for my apartment, my bed, my telephone, my comforts. I was anxious to see the morning mail.

Checks had probably come for me. Maybe there was a telegram.

The truth was that I had no place to go and nothing to do with myself. I hadn't slept much and I felt tired. I yearned for my bed. "Go home! Go home!" the Evil Spirit commanded. "Lie down, sleep, and rest up. Don't become a living corpse. It's nice to see such things on stage or read them in books, but if you do them in real life, you become a bum, a beggar, a forgotten man. There's no reason in the world why you should take revenge on yourself for the wrongs committed by others."

I was already in such a state that I began to look for an empty cab. One came by and I hailed it. I got in and the driver asked, "Where to?"

I wanted to give him the address of my home, but instead I said, "Kennedy Airport."

I rested my head against the cab wall and closed my eyes. In that moment I realized that to remain in New York was to do exactly what the Evil Spirit wanted. If I wished to divorce myself from Satan and his host, I had to leave my environs.

I had dealt the Evil Spirit a blow and I savored the taste of victory. No, I wanted neither Celia's nor Liza's apologies, nor their embraces. The Jew within me had been aroused. Generations of Jews cried out from within me: "Flee from this abomination! Run from the culture of Hitler and Stalin! Escape from a civilization that is a slaughterhouse and brothel! Flee from women who live like whores and demand to be loved and honored. Keep away from the abominable and from what resembles it."

And as the cab glided over the New York streets, I heard generations of Jews scolding me: "What's happened to you? What kind of mud have you fallen into? That's just the way the Nazis lived. This was what they preached. It was their wives and sweethearts who sold themselves to the

44

American soldiers for a box of chocolates, a pack of cigarettes, or a dollar.''

As the cab approached Kennedy, the driver asked me what airline I wanted and I named the first one that came to mind. I paid him, and carrying my small satchels and the two books, I went inside the terminal. I went up to a clerk who happened to be free, and when he asked me where I was going, I said, ''To Israel.''

''You have a ticket?''

''No, I want to buy one.''

''May I see your passport?''

I showed him the passport and he asked, ''Where's your luggage?''

And I replied, ''I'm carrying it in my hands.''

At the same time, I had the feeling that I was reading this out of some book. My life had turned into a story.

He filled out a ticket for me and I paid with traveler's checks. I couldn't get a direct route this time of day, but I got a ticket to Rome, where I could transfer to a flight to Tel Aviv. It was that simple.

Generations of Jews had fled from inquisitions, executioners, gallows, pyres. They had escaped to other enemies, other gallows, other inquisitions. Thank God, I had lived long enough for the Jews to have found their own home. No one was after me and I had enough money to last me for years if I didn't live like a wastrel. I knew that heavenly forces were helping me. Perhaps thousands of others like me nursed the same dreams, but they had to be satisfied with dreaming.

I wanted to board the plane as quickly as possible. I felt the need to sever myself physically from that which I despised.

I sat for a half hour inside the gate, waiting for my plane. For a while I stopped thinking about myself and my fate. I looked at the other passengers. What were their reasons for traveling? What were they seeking in Rome? Some of them were Italians, others were blond and Nordic-looking. A few of them looked like Jews. Each one had his reason, but I was sure that none of them had experienced what I had. Mine was surely a unique case. Jews had gone to Israel before, but these had been other Jews, in other circumstances. I sat there astounded that this was happening to me and wondering where I had gotten the strength to do what I was doing. It's true that I had lived through many adventures and faced many dangers during the Nazi years, but then I had been driven by need, by hunger, and by fear, and now I was doing something of my own free will. The Jew in me suddenly gained the courage to spit at all the idolatries.

After a while, I heard the boarding call. I had been assigned a seat on the aisle. I sat down, and presently a young woman took the window seat. Aha! The Devil had prepared a temptation for me. It's characteristic of Satan that he never gets tired, never capitulates. One holy book says that even when a person is on his deathbed, Satan comes and tries to lure him into atheism and blasphemy. There is far greater knowledge of mankind in this statement than in all the ponderous volumes of all the Freudians, Jungians, Adlerians.

7

At first, I didn't know whether the young woman was Jewish or not. I had decided not to speak to her. I had two precious books with me and I looked into one of them. At the same time I managed to steal glances at my neighbor. Her complexion was olive and she had black hair and dark eyes. She might have been a Jewish girl, or possibly Italian or even French. What do they call it?—the "Mediterranean type." She wore a short-sleeved dress cut quite low. She held a crocodile-skin handbag on her lap. I noticed a ring with a big diamond on her finger. She also carried a fashion magazine and some kind of university edition. You didn't need special powers of observation to figure out that this was what they call an intelligent person. She quickly buried herself in the book and I noticed that she was reading something by Sartre, the alleged French philosopher, writer, and formulator of existentialism, which no one understands since it is so vague and full of contradictions. Aha, so you seek the answer to the eternal questions, I thought to myself. Or maybe you need this material for a thesis.

I leafed through *The Path of the Righteous,* and even as I tasted the sanctity and wisdom of this holy book, part of my brain conjectured about the female next to me. If a dying man can think about idolatry, why can't a newly minted penitent wonder about a female? The Devil within me said: "If Moshe Haim Luzzatto himself were sitting here, he might entertain some lusty thoughts, too. He was still a young man when he died, and who persecuted him? Those so-called pious Jews, God's Cossacks." She smelled of eau de Cologne, chocolate, and other scents enticing to a male. I was reading about abstinence and sacred matters, and a corner of my brain fantasized about striking up an acquaintance with her and going with her to a hotel in Rome. I recalled the expression "a vessel of shame and disgrace." Yes, that's what the body was—a vessel of degradation. I remember my father once quoting to me from a rabbi. That rabbi—I don't recall who it was—once said: "The Evil Spirit is so brazen he would urge a venerable rabbi in a white robe to have an affair with a married woman."

I made a solemn vow to myself not to address her, not even to look at her. Soon the airplane would be taking off, and the frightful possibility existed that in ten minutes we would both be in the other world. Disasters occurred frequently and people were crushed or burned within seconds. As eager as today's man is for the material pleasures, so does he constantly risk his life—just because of these pleasures. He literally lays down his life for the merest chance of enjoyment. Well, but the passengers weren't thinking of this. They chatted, prepared to order drinks, leaned back against little pillows. Others glanced at the afternoon newspaper, at the stock-market quotations. The stewardesses, dressed in such a way as to arouse the male passengers, smiled mockingly. They revealed everything that could be revealed and promised joys—which are no joys at all.

Suddenly my neighbor glanced at my book and asked, "Is that Hebrew?"

"Yes, Hebrew," I replied.

"That's not a modern book," she observed.

"No, it's a religious work."

"Are you a rabbi?" she asked.

"No, I'm no rabbi."

"I'm Jewish, too," she said, "but I don't know any Hebrew. My parents sent me to Sunday school but I've forgotten everything. Even the alphabet. Please let me take a look."

She took *The Path of the Righteous* and I noticed that her fingernails were red as blood and sharp as a bird of prey's. It seemed to me that *The Path of the Righteous* was resentful toward me for handing it over to her.

She gazed a long time at the letters and said, "That's an aleph."

"Yes, an aleph."

"And what's this?"

"A mem."

"Right, a mem. I'm going to Israel and I must learn Hebrew. They tell me it's one of the hardest languages."

"It's not easy, but it can be learned."

"A European language is easy for me," she said. "I was in Spain for four weeks and I quickly picked up the language. But Hebrew is a completely strange element to me."

"No matter how strange an element may be, it can become familiar," I said. At the same time I knew that my words carried a sly reference, as if to say, "Now I'm a stranger, but tomorrow I may sleep with you."

She glanced at me curiously, as if she perceived my intention. Her rouged lips said, "Yes, I understand."

We got to talking. I had already forgotten about *The Path of the Righteous* and *The Voice of Elijah*. I had just fled from worldliness, but I was again a worldly person. The airplane taxied down the runway, and through the window I saw the lights rushing backwards. In a few seconds we would know whether we would live or be crushed. We were in the power of a machine and all its nuts, bolts, and gears. Thank God, the plane took off safely. I could already see the rooftops through the fog. But no one here thanked the Almighty. The passengers kept conversing as usual.

The girl told me that her fiancé had obtained a year's contract to teach electronics at Jerusalem University. She praised him as an absolute genius. He had been a professor even before he got his doctorate. He had been offered a high-paying job in a noted firm, and Washington had tried to get him. She dropped names that I forgot the moment I heard them, but the gist of it all was that, at thirty-one, Bill was one of the biggest physicists in America and a true candidate for the Nobel Prize. He had already made a number of important discoveries. He had been offered a full professorship at Harvard or Princeton—I forget which—but he had allowed himself to be persuaded by an Israeli diplomat to take a post in Jerusalem for a third of the pay that he could have gotten in the States. He was taking an Ulpan course in Hebrew, since he had to know at least a minimum of the language. He wasn't a Zionist, she added, far from it. But somehow he had been intrigued by the idea of teaching and doing research in Israel. There was a younger and more serious element there; there was idealism. He came from a rich family. His father was a famous doctor, one of the most prominent in America; he had a huge yacht, a luxury apartment on Fifth Avenue, and homes in Old Greenwich and Palm Beach. Yes, her fiancé was a Jew, but until a short time ago in name only. He hadn't had the slightest interest in Jewishness. He had never even been to Sunday school. But somehow the concept of a Jewish homeland had stirred his imagination. The Israeli diplomat was a very interesting person, himself a scientist and a young man who would surely achieve a brilliant career in the future.

She put aside her book. I knew that she'd talk to me all

night, or the few hours remaining of the night, since when you go to Europe you lose a great part of the night. I had long before noted that to women talking is a strong passion, often more urgent than sex. The stewardess came and my neighbor ordered a whiskey. I hesitated a moment, then ordered a whiskey, too. Liquor isn't forbidden, after all. The greatest rabbis took a drink. Besides, it wouldn't be polite to abstain while she drank. I wanted to show her that I was a man of the world.

We drank the strong alcohol, mine mixed with soda, hers straight. She didn't even grimace. Then she resumed talking. Her father was a lawyer. He had been divorced from her mother. He wasn't a poor man either, but hardly as rich as Bill's father. But her mother had remarried and her stepfather was a millionaire. What was her name? Priscilla. What did she do? She was interested in psychology, in literature, in sociology. How did she meet Bill? Actually, through this diplomat. He was a friend of a boyfriend of hers. They had met at a cocktail party.

She spoke in the smooth manner of those whose youth has been spent without worries, in an atmosphere of luxury, education, flirtation, and casual friendships. She wasn't rich, but she would inherit a fortune from her stepfather. He had no children, he would leave everything to Priscilla's mother, and she, in turn, would leave everything to her only daughter. Actually, her mother had been against her going to Jerusalem, especially since Bill wasn't ready to marry. But the truth was that she, Priscilla, wasn't yet ready to settle down either. What was the hurry? She wasn't particularly eager to have children, especially in light of the exploding population.

She smiled, showing her stained teeth. She ordered another whiskey and began to question me. Who was I? What did I do? Why was I going to Israel?

I told her, "I simply want to see the land of our ancestors."

"A valid reason," she observed.

I told her that I had gone through the Hitler war and hunger and wanderings in Russia. She heard me out and said, "My God, the things a person can survive!"

She asked me if I was married and I said, "I used to be."

And I put both the books in my satchel as if thinking that no matter what I said, or what happened, they shouldn't be witness to it.

8

After we had eaten a supper that arrived only three hours or so before breakfast would be served, it became half dark in the plane. The passengers settled back on their pillows, covered themselves with blankets, and got ready to sleep or doze through the curtailed night. My neighbor did the same. It was hard to tell whether she was asleep or just thinking. At least she was silent. But this didn't last more than ten minutes and she soon got her tongue back. What's more, she now spoke in a low, confidential tone. She complained, "It never occurred to me that I'd be going to Israel. I'd be less surprised if I were going to Afghanistan. I've never really identified with Jews. Neither my mother nor my father showed the slightest interest in their heritage. It's true that they sent me for a short time to Sunday school, but this was only because it was considered fashionable to be connected, no matter how superficially, with religion. The fact is that I've been ashamed of my Jewishness since childhood. All of a sudden I'm going to Israel and I'll have to learn Hebrew there. The funniest part of it all is that Bill is a total atheist."

"Israel is no more religious a country than America or France," I pointed out.

"Yes, but still—it is a Jewish country. And as for the Hebrew! I'm convinced beforehand that I will never learn it."

"Even some Arabs speak Hebrew."

"Arabs are half Jews, after all."

After a while, the conversation again reverted to private matters, and Priscilla began to expound the fact that the whole institution of marriage was stale. How could you make a contract to love someone for a lifetime? What worth did a rabbi's or a priest's blessing have anyway? The world moved forward, people lived by scientific knowledge, not by traditions that were thousands of years old. God hadn't revealed Himself to anyone, and no one knew what it was He wanted, or if He existed altogether.

I asked her, "Assuming you are right, what about the children? They need a mother and a father. The father himself has to be sure that the child is his, not his neighbor's."

Priscilla replied, "Oh, when a couple decides to have children, the woman—unless she is a monster or a lunatic—wouldn't present the man with someone else's child. But this doesn't prove that you must be faithful to someone for a lifetime."

After a while she added, "Take me and Bill, for instance. We are great friends and we intend to become husband and wife and have a child, or even two children, one day. But in the meantime, we're free and we aren't tied to each other. He goes out with other women and I go out with other men."

"What guarantee have you that he isn't sleeping with them?"

"None whatsoever."

"What guarantee has he that you won't do the same?"

"He doesn't have one and he mustn't have one. He

doesn't consider me a piece of his property. We're both free agents, that's why our marriage will be a free one, not held together by false bonds."

I knew very well that this was the Evil Spirit talking through her. There was no reason whatsoever why she should confide in me this way. You see me. I'm not handsome and I don't have the figure of a ladies' man. To you, perhaps the expression "Evil Spirit" has no more than a symbolic meaning, but to me, both the Evil Spirit and the Good Spirit are real, the very essence of reality. It isn't important whether I consider them spirits or other beings. The important thing is that they do exist and that they exert an effect on man virtually from the cradle to the grave, particularly the Evil Spirit, who has the strength of iron. Flesh, blood, nerves, and emotions are all on his side. In this world, where it takes a year to build a house and a minute to wreck it, the Evil Spirit is the master. He has all the means at his command, all the powers of destruction. If he needed a Priscilla to do his bidding, he promptly came up with one.

Yes, I knew all this, but at the same time the Evil One urged me: "Here is your chance. Don't be an idiot! Take advantage of it—the wench is willing. Such opportunities don't come up often."

I sat there baffled by the dramatic turn of events my life had taken and by my own lack of character. I had abandoned everything to flee from the lie, but the lie now sat next to me, promising me who knows what joys. I had stolen several glances at her knees and imagined all kinds of delights reposing between them. Well, but how would I go about it? Sin, too, requires time. Until we got to talking it over, it would be daytime and they'd be serving breakfast. Once in Rome, we'd probably be assigned different seats. She certainly didn't want to continue the affair with me in Israel, where her fiancé, the professor, was waiting for her. I suddenly felt as if I were merely a spectator at a play or a film in which I was also the actor. I sat still and just let things happen. I was overcome by that kind of fatalism that is not faith, but the opposite. I was half resigned and half curious to see how the director of this drama would bring all the factors together, if that was his intention.

For a long time, Priscilla didn't speak either. Then she asked, "Why don't you get a blanket? It's getting cold."

At that moment, a steward came over and asked if I wanted a blanket. I said yes, and a few seconds later my lap was covered. I don't remember where I had read—maybe in one of your stories—that man plays chess with his destiny. Man makes one move, fate makes another, and so on, until he is checkmated and the pieces are scattered. Wasn't this in one of your stories?

You see! I sat there and asked myself, What now? What's the next move? I'm not aggressive by nature. Another man in my place mightn't have hesitated another moment. He would touch her and the rest would take its natural course. But somehow I don't have this in me, thank God. I was still restrained by that Jewish sense of shame which is actually a moral force. I can't be brazen. I've avoided many pitfalls this way, but at the time, I knew that because of my shyness I had lost many rare opportunities.

I'll cut it short. All of sudden I felt her hand under my blanket. Our fingers met and the old game of squeezing, stroking, and petting commenced. Since it was she who had made the first move, I grew bolder. I put my hand on her knees—those knees that had promised me all the pleasures of this world. Needless to say, she offered no resistance. At the same time I knew that whoever might have been sitting in my place that night would have received the same favors. This woman apparently followed the theory that one mustn't pass up any opportunity, or as the Yiddish expression goes: "Let it be from a Cossack as long as it is for life." Not only did I break and defile my supposed repentance, my new way of life, and my most sacred resolutions, I also abandoned my masculine pride. I was fondling a depraved female who would give herself to anybody. Even as I fumbled with her dress and stockings I thought with a mocking sense of pity about the professor, Bill, who was waiting for this "bargain" in Jerusalem and who planned to build a family with her. The Pentateuch promised the Jews that no matter where they were dispersed, God would gather them and bring them back to the land that He had promised their ancestors. Yes, God had kept His word, but whom had He gathered? He had exiled sin and He was regathering filth.

These were my approximate thoughts, but my actions were of another sort altogether. It's hard to sin physically on an airplane. Passengers kept going to and from the rest rooms, the stewardesses weren't sleeping, the lights weren't completely extinguished, only dimmed. I felt some passion for this female, but I also felt revulsion. It's odd, but although modern woman is ready to commit all kinds of abominations, nevertheless she girds herself in such a thorough fashion that it's a struggle to get at her. The desire to appear slim is even stronger than the urge to sin. We fumbled around this way for many minutes. At the same time, we both trembled lest someone see what we were trying to do and make a scandal. It seems that the Evil Spirit or Satan was anxious to show someone in Heaven that all my vows and resolutions had been worthless, but it wasn't important to his scheme that I garner satisfaction. It is always this way with all passions. The actual deed is nothing in comparison to the anticipation. That's how it is with adultery, with theft, with murder, with a craze for honors or for revenge. There is always a letdown. I don't have to tell *you* about that.

It's getting late and I won't be able to finish my story today. But I'll add only one more fact.

After we realized that what we were trying to do wouldn't work out, we were left sitting there like two whipped dogs, ashamed before each other. At least, that's the way I felt. Things began to stir on the plane. Day was breaking outside. The sun rose from the sea all red and rinsed. I weighed my insignificance against its enormity. It illuminated planets, made grain grow, gave life to countless creatures, and did it all with purity and a divine calm, while I had tried to steal some petty and questionable pleasure and had failed. My journey had now become as meaningless as everything else about me.

I began to think about buying a ticket back to New York when I got to Rome. Since I couldn't be a Jew, I must be a pagan. Since I couldn't live in purity, I must sink deeper into the slime. Suddenly a man walked by me. He wore a rabbinical hat, had a wide blond beard, long earlocks, and the front of his coat was open to display a ritual garment with fringes. My neighbor looked at him and grimaced. Her eyes reflected embarrassment and scorn. I realized at that moment that without earlocks and a ritual garment one cannot be a real Jew. A soldier who serves an emperor has to have a uniform, and this also applies to a soldier who serves the Almighty. Had I worn such an outfit that night, I wouldn't have been exposed to those temptations. The way a person dressed expresses a resolution, and an obligation to the Kingdom of Heaven. Such is the nature of man that he is more ashamed of his fellow man than he is of God. If he doesn't display a sign, if he doesn't broadcast to the whole world who and what he is, he leaves himself open to transgressions that cannot be resisted.

9

*In Rome, we had about a three-hour wait for the plane to Is-*rael. My new friend didn't have the patience to sit in the airport and wait. I saw a young man offer to give her a quick tour of the city. He promised to bring her back in time. These kind of people strike up fast acquaintanceships. I sat down on a bench. I hadn't eaten much, since I couldn't get kosher food on the plane and had become a vegetarian besides. But I wasn't hungry. I watched the crowds. I listened to the announcements made in Italian and English. I observed the people coming and going. Some were going to Paris, some to New York, some to London, and some to Athens. Their eyes displayed the same restlessness, the same sense of urgency, and the same queries: Why am I running like this? What am I seeking? What do I expect to find there?

A passenger had lost his baggage and was complaining bitterly. The officials wouldn't hear him out and they shuttled him from one to the other. Problems and failure had no room in a system where everything must operate with the precision of a fine watch. A person with complaints was a misfit and a burden.

During this whole time a force spoke within me: "Since you've defiled everything and broken all your resolutions, where are you running? What will you do in Israel?" But despite this, I stayed put and waited for my plane. I had no one and nothing to go back to. After a while, I went into a restaurant and ordered dry toast and tea. I ate, drank, and thought about suicide. Since I couldn't live, I should die. But I wasn't ready for death. I sat there till it was time to leave. When I came to the gate from which the plane left for Israel, I noticed the man in the rabbinical hat and earlocks whom I had seen previously on the plane. He had several yeshiva students with him. They were dressed more or less like him, but their earlocks were even longer. People stared at them with mocking glances, but apparently these youths didn't care in the slightest what others thought of them.

I cocked my ears and listened. They were talking about some rabbi and recalling a subject they had all studied. They spoke the kind of Yiddish I had heard at the old rabbi's house in New York.

How did they become what they are, I wondered. How did they decide at such a young age what I still couldn't decide after so many disappointments, so much introspection and suffering? Weren't they subject to temptations? Were they born holy? I had the urge to speak to one of them, but they were busy with the older man, who I gathered was the head of a yeshiva. He held a book in his hand and from time to time he opened it as if resenting every moment away from it. Obviously, the Torah and good deeds represented to him and to his disciples not simply a duty or a burden that they had assumed but great exaltation. There was something akin to passion in their eyes—a thirst for the Torah, a fervor to serve the Almighty, to carry out all His commandments and to assume even more rigors and restrictions, thus denying the Devil the slightest access to them.

Yes, restrictions do serve as barriers. If someone has a treasure that he doesn't want stolen, he hides it in a place inaccessible to thieves and robbers. If he fears that one lock isn't enough, he affixes two locks. If he suspects that someone may try to tunnel toward them, he'll post a guard. Think of the many restrictions assumed by those who are concerned with literature, theater, music, fashions, women, or other worldly passions. I read somewhere that Flaubert never repeated a word within the same chapter. There are rich and elegant women who won't wear the same dress twice. Yes, worldliness is full of restrictions, too (or maybe I should apologize for using the comparison). They squander thousands, they sacrifice themselves because of these worldly pedantries. But when these same people meet an observant Jew, they start asking such questions as: "Where does it say in the Torah that you mustn't trim the beard?" "Where does it say that you must wear a long gaberdine?" They forget or make themselves forget that trimming the beard and wearing modern clothing is a compromise with worldliness, an attempt to mimic the Gentile or the Jewish Gentile. The Torah says, "After the doings of the land of Egypt shall ye not do . . . and in their ordinances shall ye not walk." According to the Gemara, you may not even tie your shoelaces the same way the idolators do. Without these determents, you open the door to evil. Just as fads constantly change among the pagans, so must the true Jew constantly assume new rigors and restraints.

I often heard worldly Jews ask, "How do you know that Jacob or Moses wore a satin gaberdine on the Sabbath?"

I say to them, "Moses didn't imitate the idol worshippers of his time and we mustn't imitate the idol worshippers of our time.'' If it should ever happen that the worldly put on satin gaberdines, then the pious Jews would wear jackets.

It took me a long time to understand this basic truth, but I began to understand it on that morning in the Rome airport.

Soon it was time to board. This time, I got a seat next to some old woman who wasn't going to Israel but to Greece. After a while, I had to go to the toilet. I looked around and saw Priscilla deeply engrossed in conversation with the same young man who showed her around. She was so absorbed that she didn't even see me. She had already forgotten me and was concentrating on this other fellow. Had it been dark and had they been covered with a blanket, she would have tried to do the same with him as she had with me. This is the substance of the worldly woman. Not all of them go to such extremes, but their philosophy is the same: Snatch it all while you can!

I can't say that my arrival in Israel had the same effect on me as it had had on Rabbi Nachman of Bratzlav, or on others of lesser stature. The airport in Israel had nothing particularly Jewish about it. True, the signs were in Hebrew and the announcements in that language, too, but modern Hebrew has lost much of the Jewish flavor, the Jewish uniqueness, the Jewish scorn for worldly illusions. Modern Hebrew is one hundred percent worldly. It's Hebrew, but it's no longer the Sacred Tongue. A language used to build ships and airplanes and to manufacture guns and bombs cannot be a Sacred Tongue. Modern Hebrew has swallowed up the old Sacred Tongue.

I stood in line and waited for the official to stamp my passport. Naturally he was a Jew, not a Gentile. His eyes reflected a trace of our heritage. But just a trace. The modern Jew's yearning to be like a Gentile is directly contrary to the essence of Jewishness, which is to be as distant from the Gentile as it's possible to get. I spoke with many of these Israelis and they nearly all said the same thing: The Diaspora has failed; the Diaspora has been one long mistake, and similar such talk. But what would have happened to the Jews if they hadn't experienced the Diaspora? They would have blended in with the nations. We wouldn't have been only dispersed physically but annihilated forever. A number of the Nazis undoubtedly stemmed from Jews who converted during the time of Mendelssohn and later. It's just one step from assimilation to conversion, and sometimes no more than a generation or two from conversion to Nazism.

I know what you want to say: "Tell the story, don't preach." No, I'm not preaching. I don't want to change you. But I can't tell you this story if I don't express my feelings to you.

I went up to the window, the official stamped my passport, and I went outside. A taxi came up and I told the driver to take me to Tel Aviv. When he asked what hotel I wanted, I told him to take me to the nearest one. I looked out of the taxi window at the land of the Pentateuch and of our ancestors. It was much warmer here than in New York. The day was mild, the sky was bluish, with just a few clouds. Neither the country nor its climate was a disappointment to me, but still it wasn't the Israel of the spirit. The people were the exact replica of those I had seen fifteen hours before in New York. They were dressed in Gentile fashion and they looked like Gentiles. Their faces reflected the same impatience, the same sense of worldly rush and greed. Another taxi tried to outrace us and it was only by an eyelash that both cars didn't turn over. My driver cursed the other driver in Hebrew and shook his fist at him. We drove into Tel Aviv. We passed a movie theater, and the signs displayed flashy actresses and wild-faced men with guns. They played the same trash here as in New York. When we passed a bookstore, I saw the same cheap novels as in New York. The driver had taken me to the Hotel Dan. I might just as well as have been in some hotel on Broadway.

I wasn't then, and I'm still not, one to lay the blame on others. You cannot create a kingdom of priests and a holy nation these days. We couldn't even build one in the days of Joshua, the son of Nun.

Those who say that the Exile was a failure don't realize that from Moses' standpoint, the Land of Israel was a failure, too. The people there began to mingle with the idol worshippers from the very first. The idols and the harlots emerged immediately. The Scriptures say about nearly every king: "And he did not what was right in the sight of the Lord." Jews forgot the Torah so completely during the time of Josiah that it had to be rediscovered again.

It's getting late and I must stop, but before I go, I want to say just one more thing to you: The Jew has attained his highest degree of spirituality only in the time of the Diaspora. The Scriptures were a great beginning, an enormous foundation, but the Jews of the Scriptures were, with few exceptions, still half Gentiles. The Mishnah represented a tremendous step forward and the Gemara went even further. It took many generations for an Isaac Luria, a Baal Shem Tov, a Vilna Gaon, a Kozhenitz Preacher, a Seer of Lublin, and in later times a Chofetz Chaim and others like them to evolve. Those who want to turn the Jews back to Scripture would wreck the Jewish building and leave only the foundation. That head of the yeshiva and his students whom I met in the Rome airport are Jewry's greatest achievement. They have isolated themselves from the worldliness more than any other Jews in our history. They were exactly that which Moses demanded: a holy people, guarded by a thousand restraints, a people which "shall dwell alone and shall not be reckoned among the nations." True, they are no more than a small minority, but great ideals have never become mass movements.

* * *

Joseph Shapiro glanced at his watch. "Oh, it's late! It's time I went home. If you want to hear more of my story we can meet again tomorrow."

"Yes, I do. Let's meet tomorrow."

The
Second
Day

10

I thought that those I'd left in New York would look for me and find me in Israel. I wasn't traveling on a false passport and the police could easily have tracked me down. But apparently Celia had accepted the idea that everything was over between us. I assumed that she could collect alimony from me and who knows what else. That's how the Gentile and the Jewish-Gentile laws are—they favor the guilty. The judge, the criminal, and the defense attorneys are often part and parcel of the same institution. They can easily exchange positions. They read the same books, they attend the same nightclubs, they often go out with the same kind of women. Few of them have regard for justice or faith in a higher power. But so far no one had bothered me and I was able to wander freely through Tel Aviv.

In the first days, I didn't seek out any acquaintances. I wanted to be alone and to take stock—for perhaps the first time—of my life. I strolled along Ben Yehuda Street, went to Dizengoff Boulevard for a cup of coffee, and watched the other idlers who sat at the tables outside, chattered endlessly, read newspapers, and looked at the passersby. When a good-looking woman walked by, the men's eyes lit up as if they were starved for sex and hadn't been with a woman for ages. Their hungry gazes seemed to me to be asking: *Maybe? . . . Maybe this is the one I've been dreaming of . . . Perhaps chance will bring us together and it will be the beginning of that great happiness that writers describe in books . . .* This sudden-born hope would last until the woman turned the corner into Frishman Street or I. L. Gordon Street and then the potential Don Juans turned back to their wrinkled newspapers and their cigarette butts. The women who sat at the tables also looked at the passing women and made all kinds of snide remarks: this one had fat legs, that one's hips were too wide, that one dressed in bad taste . . . The store windows displayed dresses, jackets, lingerie in the latest style. The Language Committee had already found Hebrew words for all the knickknacks sold here. Whatever else he may be, modern man isn't ever at a loss for words. I was sitting near a bookstore and from time to time I glanced at the window. All the kitsch novels in the world had already been translated into the Holy Tongue. The kiosks displayed posters advertising cheap plays. If not for the Hebrew characters, I might have been in Paris, Madrid, Lisbon, or Rome. Yes, the Enlightened have attained their goal. We are a people like all other peoples. We feed our souls the same dung as they do. We're already raising our daughters to be depraved. We already publish Hebrew magazines that describe in detail which Hollywood harlot slept with what Hollywood pimp.

There was one café here where writers and maybe actors and actresses congregated. I occasionally looked in there. In my younger years I had entertained certain notions about writers and writing. I read their books. I was inspired by the way they could put into words so many thoughts and feelings, often the hiddenmost emotions of the human heart. But as they sat there, their faces expressed the same greed, shallowness, and vanity as the others. They became just as aroused when some female flounced by. Their wives uttered the same petty remarks, while they took sips of their lemonade or orange drink with their rouged lips. You didn't need any special talent to note that the female intellectuals nursed the same illusions, the same unattainable urges, the same dreams about a happiness that doesn't exist, as did the other, non-creative people. Between one fantasy and the other, they read some ridiculous story about a beauty pursued by millionaires, or an actress who got ten thousand dollars a night to sing in Las Vegas. From time to time they glanced at themselves in mirrors. Was their age showing? Had they managed to erase every trace of wrinkles? Was Helena Rubinstein's cream really capable of halting the erosions wrought by time?

After several days of being alone, I began to look up acquaintances from Warsaw—friends, half friends, people I had met in Vilna, in Moscow, in Tashkent. I had no need to look for them, for as soon as one found out that I was here, he told the others. I met some of them sitting there in the cafés on Dizengoff Boulevard. The kissing began and the honeyed words, the questions, the reminiscences. Many of our mutual friends had perished under Hitler, or starved to death, or died in Stalin's prisons, or been killed serving in the Red Army or in the Polish resistance. Some had died of cancer or a heart attack. Well, no matter how many had died, there were always some left. All Tel Aviv was one big survival camp. I constantly heard the words *died, perished, shot, killed.* The widowers had new wives, the widows new husbands. Those women who were young enough had borne new children.

I was inundated with invitations. I was constantly buying flowers and candy and taking cabs. Some of the people I met told me that they had already considered me among the dead. I had reappeared like a resurrected corpse. From the way I was dressed and from the presents I brought, they presumed that I wasn't a pauper back home in New York. Some even began to hint or ask openly that I help bring them to America. Certainly, Israel was our country and our hope, but it was hard to digest so much of the Holy Tongue, so much Jewishness. You couldn't work your way up here—it was whispered—you couldn't get anywhere without "pull" or protection. You had to belong to the right party and know people in power. Like everywhere else, here, too, might was right. Could it be otherwise? Jews are people, after all.

One of the women I met spoke to me of intimate matters. She said that the climate here cooled a man's ardor during the heat waves and worked exactly opposite on women, who became consumed with passion.

"What do you do about it?"

"Oh, we manage."

And she smiled a sly smile. I saw that she herself was ready to "manage," actually with me. Why not? I was a tourist, an American, I wouldn't spread any gossip about her. I lived in a good hotel, I wasn't stingy or poor. She volunteered a lot of information. She knew all about my acquaintances, their comings and goings, their family life, even their secret desires. She kept repeating that even here in the Holy Land people didn't behave any more circumspectly than they did in Paris or New York. I realized that not everything she told me was necessarily so, but I later heard the same things from others. No, Hebrew characters and Jewish leaders did not serve as barriers against iniquity.

Between one meeting and another, between one invitation and the next, I would steal into a synagogue. True, many Jews do pray in Tel Aviv. Many lead pure and decent lives. The schools teach the children the Scripture, Jewish history, the Mishnah, and an occasional bit of the Gemara. Many observe the Sabbath and eat kosher food. But the more closely I watched these Jews, the more clearly I felt that they lacked the power to keep their children from the worldliness

72

that ruled the land. This was not, in most cases, a Jewishness born of great faith, but a routine, and occasionally an
obligation based on party membership. It was a cold or luke-
warm Jewishness. In the synagogues I spoke to the worshippers. None of them possessed the kind of faith that can
overcome the fires of the Evil Spirit. They concluded their
prayers and the beadle locked the doors. I found no study
houses here where boys sat chanting the Talmud as they
once did in Warsaw or Lublin. The boys with tiny skullcaps
perched on the tips of their heads, the fathers with trimmed
beards (or clean-shaven with depilatory), the mothers without wigs were fine enough people, but not fighters against
Satan. They belonged to the religious party. Both their sons
and their daughters served in the army. They generally read
the same newspapers as did the non-observers and attended
the same movies. Day in, day out, they absorbed more and
more worldliness into themselves, along with all the world's
ambitions. Many of the men prayed only on the Sabbaths
and holidays. I came to the conclusion that they had barely
enough strength to maintain this observance through a few
generations.

But I wasn't concerned about them, only about myself. I
had fled from Celia and Liza but I was again surrounded by
countless Celias and Lizas, real ones and potential ones. I
knew that from all these invitations and meetings with female friends would come the sort of life that I was trying to
escape. I already had offers of an affair from a few married
women. The faith that had been ignited within me during the
worst crisis of my life began to cool and grow extinguished.
I stood in the synagogue ostensibly praying, but the words
had ceased to comfort and convince me. I mumbled the
Eighteen Benedictions and each benediction seemed a lie.
Not even the slightest proof existed that God would resur-
rect the dead, heal the sick, punish the wicked, reward the
just. Six million Jews had been burned, tortured, obliter-
ated. Tens of millions of enemies lurked over the State of Is-

rael ready to lay waste that which Hitler had left untouched. Former Nazis in Germany drank beer and spoke openly about new massacres. In Russia and in America, there grew a generation that had forgotten Jewishness and had become fully or partly atheistic. Many Jews throughout the world served the leftist idolatries, followed all the foolish fads and false theories. They had become more worldly than the worldliest, often more pagan than the pagans. Even if there was a God who *could* send a Messiah, there were few for whom to send him . . .

With such thoughts in my mind, I prayed. With such thoughts in my mind, I went to sleep and I got up again.

11

I almost remained in Tel Aviv with a new sweetheart, or maybe with two. But some force kept reminding me about the reason I was here and about that from which I had fled. The Jewish spark, or the voice from Mount Horeb, wouldn't let me sink again into the illusions of the material world. The voice would suddenly ask me: "Is this why you fled, to rise from one dungheap and fall into another?" The voice also argued: "If you, Joseph Shapiro, heir of scholars and saintly women, are ready to break the Ten Commandments, what can you expect from the sons and daughters of generations of evildoers and idol worshippers?" The men with whose wives I was contemplating affairs had been victims of Hitler. They had lost families in Poland. They had remarried in Israel and were anxious to begin new lives. Did I really want to steal their wives, to buy them with money and presents? I wouldn't be able to live with myself if I committed such a crime. I would consider myself a Nazi.

I had heard a lot about the kibbutzim. One day I took a

trip to a kibbutz where a distant relative of mine lived. It was a leftist kibbutz. I brought a gift for my relative and he was delighted to get it. He showed me everything: the school, the cowshed, the barn, the lake where carp were hatching. There was a handsome building there called the Culture House. I was supposed to spend the night at the kibbutz, and my relative, an old member, gave me his room. There was voting that night, and all the members attended a meeting after dinner. I saw that the lights were on in the Culture House and I went inside. I was told that there was a library with newspapers from Israel and other countries. When I stepped inside I found it empty. The lights were on but there was no one there. I glanced up at the wall and saw a picture of Lenin and one of Stalin. What Stalin had done, how many Jews he had exterminated, and what a terrible enemy of Israel he was were well-known facts, but there hung his portrait anyway. The leftist Jews of that kibbutz weren't yet ready to divorce themselves from this architect of "progress," this prophet of a "bright tomorrow" and a "better future." I felt like tearing the picture off the wall, trampling and spitting on it. Newspapers lay on the table, among them Soviet ones, as well as Communist and leftist newspapers and magazines in a number of languages, including Yiddish.

As I sat there rummaging through the papers, a girl came in, apparently a member of the kibbutz. She glanced at me with some surprise. I wasn't in any mood to converse and I kept reading some article in a Red sheet that tried to prove that the only salvation for the world was Communism. The girl began to leaf through a leftist magazine, too, a Hebrew one. I had the feeling that she was waiting for someone. From time to time she glanced toward the door.

Yes, a young man did come in presently. He had black, curly hair and shining black eyes. They were apparently both convinced that I, an American, couldn't understand a word of Hebrew. First, they talked about me. The young man asked who I was and she said, "The devil knows— some American tourist who happened by."

After a while, they began discussing more intimate matters, and although it wasn't easy for me to decipher all the words spoken in the Sephardic pronunciation, I gathered the gist of what they were saying. She had a husband who had gone to Jerusalem but she didn't know if he would be back this night or in the morning. The young man proposed that she come to his place, but she said that this was too risky. Yes, here in this Culture House in this kibbutz you could establish the same cheating contacts that you could in all other such houses among both Jews and Gentiles. Stalin's portrait on the wall and the conversation of these two young people convinced me once and for all that you couldn't find any more feeling for Jewishness among the worldly Jews of Israel than you could among the worldly Jews in other countries. The modern Jew harbored all the lies and delusions of his time. What he called culture was actually a lack of culture, the law of the jungle. True, in the other kibbutzim they had already removed Stalin's portrait, or maybe they hadn't hung it up in the first place, but even there they placed their hopes on flimsy sociology, on false psychology, on fatuous poetry, on the interpretations of Karl Marx, Freud, this professor or that professor. They always dragged down old idols and replaced them with new ones. They placed all their hopes on officials whose convictions, politics, and concepts of justice changed with every passing breeze. One day these leaders were the warmest of friends; the next, deadly enemies. One day they cut each other up, and the next they gave each other banquets, drank toasts, and bedecked each other with medals.

Although the Jewish political leaders strove to be exactly as diplomatic and dialectical as the Gentile—this didn't diminish the age-old hatred of the Jews. No matter how much the Jew has tried to imitate the Gentile, he had remained alien and despised. He still could not be forgiven the sin of not cutting himself off completely from his old heritage, his "arrogance" at refusing to integrate fully with those who burned his holy books and murdered his children. In their hatred of the Jews, there was no difference between the Hitlers and the Stalins.

That night, I slept in the kibbutz. I had passed by the building where the meeting was being held and I overheard an old comrade accuse the audience of having cooled on the socialist ideals and of leaning toward nationalism. He spoke with fervor, he ranted, he slammed his fist against the table. He called the rabbis in Israel reactionary clericals, black crows who wanted to turn back the wheels of history. I wanted to ask him, "Where do the wheels of history lead? How can you be so sure that the wheels of history won't get bogged down in blood and marrow again?" But I went to sleep instead.

Sleep—that's a joke. Actually I hardly slept that night. I seemed to see Jews digging their own graves while the Nazis stood around and drove them on with whips: "Faster! Deeper!" I saw them lead Jewish men and women to the ovens. I saw drunken Germans torturing Jews with every possible method devised by that "distinguished author," the Marquis de Sade, and by other such "greats." They were all integral parts of the worldly culture—Hitler and Stalin, Napoleon and Bismarck, all the whores, pimps, pornographers, all those who threw bombs, carried out raids, sent whole peoples to Siberia or to the gas chambers. Even Al Capone and Jack the Ripper were part of this culture. There isn't a scoundrel about whom the professors don't write books, do research into his psychological make-up, provide countless excuses for his deeds . . .

That night, I came to the final conclusion that not only must I abandon the culture that had spawned and justified all this evil and falseness but I must also turn to the very opposite of it. I must become someone as far removed from this kind of culture as our grandfathers had been. I must become that which they had been: Talmud Jews, Jews of the Gemara, of the Midrash, of Rashi, of the Zohar, of *The Beginning of Wisdom,* of *The Two Tablets of the Covenant.* Only such a Jew is separated from the wicked. The slightest compromise that you make with the pagan culture of our time is a gesture toward evil, a nod to a world of murder, idolatry, and adultery.

I must confess that at the time that I made this resolve, my faith wasn't yet that strong. I was still completely riddled with doubt and with what I might even call heresy. I went away from evil, you might say, not so much out of love for Mordecai as out of hate for Haman. I was filled with a raging disgust against the world and against the civilization of which I was a part. I ran like a beast runs from a forest fire, like a man fleeing from a pursuing enemy.

The very first thing the next morning I took the bus to Jerusalem.

12

I wandered through the narrow streets of Jerusalem. This was long before the Six-Day War. Old Jerusalem was still in the hands of the Arabs and it seemed that we would never get it back. But Meah Shearim was ours and that is where I went. And as I walked along, the Evil One harangued me: "Joseph Shapiro, where are you going? Those Jews believe every word in the Shulhan Arukh, while your head is filled with what the Bible critics wrote and the materialists preached. You can no more become one of the pious than you can become a Turk." But I kept on going. I came to a building and saw a house of prayer. It was a study house of the Sandzer Hasidim.

Before I go on, I must tell you that during my week and a half in Tel Aviv I had encountered quite a bit of snobbism toward me and my kind. Those born in Israel, the so-called Sabras, consider us Diaspora Jews aliens, especially if we don't speak Hebrew with their pronunciation and with all the new words they've invented. The leftist Jews disdain the rightest Jews. Among the leftists themselves there are many distinctions. A member of Mapam considers a member of Mapai a reactionary. They both consider a General Zionist a bourgeois. To a Communist, they are all a bunch of fascists whom it would be a good deed to exterminate. I often heard the leftists make vicious slurs against America and American Jews. They claimed that American Jews were a bunch of moneybags and worshippers of the Golden Calf. When I reminded them that American Jews supported all the institutions in Israel, and that without them the State of Israel wouldn't exist, they replied that the American Jews gave the money to avoid taxes and were actually indifferent about Israel.

I heard many jeering attacks against the Hadassah women, against American rabbis, against everybody in general. I often thought: We are a small people, half of which has been annihilated, yet the remnant is consumed with such divisiveness, such antipathy. It struck me that if the Israeli Jews were no longer obliged to come to the American Jews for aid, they would spit in their faces.

I went inside the Sandzer study house thinking that I would feel more of a stranger here than anywhere else. I was dressed in modern fashion, I had no beard, I wore no earlocks. To these Jews, I was nothing more than a blight against Jewishness. But what happened was the very opposite. I came in and felt myself transported back to my youth. Jews like my grandfather—with gray beards, earlocks, skullcaps on their heads, and wide ritual garments with long fringes—came up and greeted me. Their eyes seemed to say: "It's true that you are alienated from us, but still you are our brother." I saw in their eyes something that I had never seen among modern Jews: love for Jewishness, love for a fellow Jew, even if he was a sinner. It wasn't a feigned love, it was real. Everyone can tell real love from fake.

Several men and youths sat at tables studying the Gemara. Some studied silently, others aloud. Some sat bent over and others swayed and their earlocks swayed along rhythmically. I saw children no more than twelve or thirteen already studying the Gemara on their own. An odd kind of nobility exuded from their faces. They didn't have to pass any tests; they didn't need the Torah for their careers. They studied because this was the reason for which the Jew had been created. They would never receive any honors for it, and chances were they would remain paupers all their lives.

I took out the tractate of Betzah and tried to study. I knew how little relevance it had, dealing with an egg that a hen laid on a holiday. Could the egg be eaten or not? The School of Shamai said yes, the House of Hillel said no. I need not tell you that all the Enlightened, all the enemies of Talmud, use this tractate as an example of how removed the Talmud is from the world, how little it has to do with logic, with the times, with social problems, and so forth and so on.

"But," I asked myself, "how is it that I feel like a stranger among modern Jews and like an intimate here?"

When the Sandzer Hasidim saw that I had taken out a book, they grew closer to me. Men came over and greeted me and asked me where I was from. When I told them from America, they began to inquire about the Jews in America as one would ask about brothers, not about "moneybags," "reactionaries," and "worshippers of the Golden Calf."

The modern Jews only wanted to favor me with their "ideals," but these Jews sought to attend to my body. They asked me where I was staying, and when I told them I hadn't yet checked into a hotel, they recommended a place where I could spend the night. Unbelievable as it may sound, several of the men invited me to their homes for dinner. I could spend the night in their homes as well, they told me. They didn't feel that one shouldn't inquire into another's private affairs. On the contrary, they asked me what I did for a living, if I was married, if I had children, and how long I planned to stay in Israel. They spoke to me as if they were my relatives. To the one who asked me if I had a wife, I lied by saying I was divorced, and he promptly proposed a match for me. Naturally, I assumed that he might be trying to earn a matchmaker's fee. A young man came up and asked me for a donation. But all this was done without superciliousness and with courtesy. Since I was a Jew who looked into a Gemara, I was one of them.

I studied a good number of pages that day. I prayed at the evening services with the men. Between one service and the next, a circle of elderly men and youths formed around me. In America, young people look upon the older person as someone to be thrown to the dogs. There is no worse insult there than to say about someone that he has aged. When parents invite a guest, their children are rarely present. Young people in America ignore their parents. I must say that I saw the same thing among the modern people in Israel. To be young for them is considered the greatest achievement.

I didn't detect a trace of this among the Sandzer Hasidim. On the contrary, the youths showed genuine rather than put-on respect toward the elderly. Modern man is a thorough believer in the material world. The elderly person has already used up a great share of this world and has little left to eat, or to fornicate. But the young man still has a large reserve, and for this alone he is entitled to respect and recognition. Besides, the young person is identified with the latest fads. He is the newness, the vogue, the progress that is the idolatry of modern man.

I spent that evening at the house of a head of a yeshiva who had invited me for dinner. I was afraid that his wife, when she saw he had brought home a guest without letting her know first, would be upset. But she was apparently used to this. I was given a skullcap and shown where to wash my hands for dinner. There was no bathroom in the apartment and the towel was not the cleanest. The mistress of the house had a wrinkled face. I gathered from her talk that she was barely past fifty. In America and even in Israel, I had seen women her age having illicit affairs, drawing alimony from husbands they had deceived, wallowing in luxury, and indulging themselves in adultery and in other wickedness. But this pious woman had long since accepted the onset of age as part of the honor of being a mother of grown children, a mother-in-law, and a grandmother. Her eyes reflected the goodness of the true Jewish mother, not the mothers mocked in books and plays, and whom American Jewish writers and some psychoanalysts consider the source of their children's nervous afflictions.

It may seem funny to you, but I fell in love with this woman. I realized that even from a romantic and sexual standpoint such a woman was more interesting than those old witches who dress like sixteen-year-olds, drink like sailors, curse like streetwalkers, and whose alleged love is in fact sheer hatred. It's no wonder that so many modern men become impotent or homosexuals. You have to have queer inclinations in the first place to marry one of these.

The man, Reb Haim, asked my reason for coming to Israel and I told him the truth: that I was disgusted by the kind of life I had been leading; that I wanted to become a Jew—a real Jew, not a nationalistic Jew or a socialist Jew, or however they call themselves.

He said, "It's a long time since I've heard such words. What do you propose to do?"

"I've saved up some money. I want to pray, to study, to be a Jew."

"Why did you pick the Sandzer study house?"

"I just happened to be passing by and I saw the study house. It was merely a coincidence."

"Coincidence? . . . *Et* . . ."

Again I heard the same expression that I had heard in the old rabbi's house in New York. These Jews didn't believe in coincidences.

After a while, he said, "Coincidence is chance. The Enlightened claim that the world is chance, but a Jew who has faith knows that everything is destined. Coincidence is not a kosher word . . .''

13

As you already know, I'm hardly an exponent of modern man and his literature, but Shakespeare's contention that all the world's a stage is a truth that is tied into faith, into the belief in Providence. Just as in a play, where the protagonist often appears in the very first scene, that's how life is, too. You come to a foreign country, to a strange city, and you immediately meet the people who will play a vital role in your life, the chief heroes of your personal drama. That's exactly what happened to me.

I sat there and ate dinner at my host's, Reb Haim's, house, and I asked him if he had any children. He sighed and told me that he had had several children, but only one daughter was still living, and she provided him no satisfaction. It seemed that one son had volunteered for the 1948 war and had been killed by an Arab bullet. Two other children had died while still young. The one remaining daughter had married a yeshiva student but he had died six months after the wedding. She had been a widow for three years. I asked him what she did, and he said she was a seamstress who lived not far away.

Just as we sat talking, the door opened and in came a young woman with a kerchief over her head. She looked no more than eighteen, but I later learned she was twenty-four. One look sufficed to tell me a lot about her: first of all, that hers was a rare beauty, not the kind fashioned in beauty parlors, but the beauty and charm that's given by God.

Secondly, I saw that she glowed with the grace of chastity. The concept that the eyes are the windows of the soul is not a mere figure of speech. You can see in a person's eyes whether he is full of arrogance or modesty, honesty or cunning, pride or humility, fear of God or abandon. This young woman's eyes reflected all that is good about the Jew. Her gaze revealed all the great qualities mentioned in *The Path of the Righteous*. When she saw me, a stranger, she took a step backwards. She seemed frightened by me.

Thirdly, I knew practically at that second that she was my destiny; that I wouldn't rest until she became my wife. Reb Haim was right—coincidence is not a kosher word. Everything that had happened had led me to this city, to this house. I had never before felt the hand of Providence so strongly.

Apparently the young woman sensed it, too, for she grew strangely disturbed, blushed, and seemed dazed.

I heard her mother ask, "Serele, why don't you say good evening? Our guest is from America."

"Good evening," Sarah said, and her voice was like an obedient child's.

"Good evening, good year," I replied.

"Serele, have you had your supper yet?" her mother asked.

"No, I'll eat later."

"Eat with us."

I was hoping that she would sit down at the table, but in this house females didn't eat at the same table with men, particularly not with strangers. Only Reb Haim and I sat at the table while the women ate in the kitchen. Fate had tossed me from Celia, Liza, and Priscilla back to the true Jewishness, to the source from which we had all drunk, back onto the path that led to the Torah and to purity. In bygone years I had seen so much wantonness, licentiousness, and adultery that I had already forgotten there were other kinds of women. Celia and Liza had often accused me of lacking respect for women. But what was there to respect about them? Celia claimed that D. H. Lawrence, the author of *Lady Chatterley's Lover,* was the greatest writer of all time. I had often found pornographic books at Liza's. Both Celia and Liza liked gangster movies. When the gangsters shot or stabbed each other, they laughed. I myself used to suffer terribly during these scenes. Violence and bloodshed have always made me shudder. Celia and Liza both loved lobster. I knew that a lobster is cooked alive in boiling water. But these supposedly delicate ladies didn't care that because of them a living creature was being murdered in a most horrible fashion. Celia and Liza both liked plays full of shocking horror and dissolution. And all this was done in the name of an art whose eternal theme is violence and fornication.

Only now as I speak to you do I realize how much suffering this art has caused me. In order to enjoy it, you must have the heart of a murderer. It is completely sadistic, mean and cruel. I often saw Celia and Liza laughing at scenes that should have evoked tears. The hero went through torture and agony, and this was supposed to be amusing. There is an expression, "gallows humor," and this is the humor of modern man. He laughs at another's misfortune. When a healthy young woman deceives an old and sick husband, this is supposedly comic. All the heroes in worldly literature have been whoremongers and evildoers. Anna Karenina, Madame Bovary, Raskolnikov, and Taras Bulba are the typical heroes and heroines of literature. Homer's *Iliad* and *Odyssey,* Dante's *Divine Comedy,* Goethe's *Faust,* right down to the trash aimed at pleasing the street louts and wenches, are full of cruelty and abandon. All worldly art is nothing but evil and degradation. Through the generations writers have glorified killing and debauchery and they have all kinds of names for it—romanticism, realism, naturalism, New Wave, and so on.

Lately, I have come to understand why pious Jews never believed, and still don't believe, in studying too much Scripture. The horror stories in the Scriptures somehow didn't befit the spirit of the Diaspora Jew. Rabbi Isaac Luria and Baal Shem Tov are closer and more understandable to him than Joshua, the son of Nun, and King David. Joshua and King David had to be justified and defended, but Rabbi Isaac Luria and Baal Shem Tov needed no defense whatsoever. For the same reasons, the Enlightened also praised those parts of the Scripture that they called "worldly." Reciting the Psalms was to them a waste of time, but to read about the Jewish wars—this was worldliness. Our fathers and grandfathers identified the Song of Songs with the Almighty, with the Divine Presence, with Israel, but the Enlightened went out of their way to prove that the Song of Songs was simply a love ballad. I'm not talking against the Scriptures, God forbid. The Scriptures are holy. But Jewishness has developed. All things start out raw, and ripen with time. When the apple is green, it doesn't have the same sweet taste as when it is ripe. The basement of a house is not as elegant as a drawing room.

I had taught myself precisely how to talk to a Celia, a Liza, or a Priscilla, but how did one speak to a Sarah? This, I had already forgotten. I took one look at her and I didn't see her again that evening, although the apartment was small. After supper, she left. She mumbled a good night to me and to her father, but she averted her face.

Reb Haim wanted me to sleep over, but I turned down his invitation. I could see that there was no room for me there. Also, I had grown unaccustomed to the old featherbeds and I was afraid there might be fleas or bedbugs in such a household. I said goodbye to Reb Haim and to his wife, Beile Brocha, and went out to find a hotel. I promised to come back the next morning to the Sandzer study house.

Reb Haim looked at me doubtfully and said, "For the sake of God, don't forget to do so."

"No, Reb Haim," I replied, "I won't part from you anymore."

I found a hotel. This was the first day that I lived like a Jew. The Evil Spirit had been silenced, but I knew that he would presently regain his tongue. Sure enough, I soon heard him say, "All this would be fine if you were a true believer, but actually, you are nothing more than a heretic afflicted with nostalgia. You will soon turn back to your heretic ways, and what's more, you'll bring nothing but grief to a pious Jewish daughter. You won't be able to stand her for long. You'll get tired of her in one month, or, at the most, three."

"I'll marry her and I'll stay with her," I said in reply to the Glib One. "I'll be a Jew whether you approve of it or not. He who despises evil must believe in holiness."

"I've seen a lot of such penitents as you," Satan countered. "It's no more than a passing fancy. They always go back to what they were."

"If I can't be a Jew, I'll put an end to my life!" I shouted within me.

"These are the words of a modern man," an imp whispered in my ear.

I went to bed, but I lay there for hours unable to sleep. I had fallen in love with Sarah, my present wife and the mother of my children.

14

That night I resolved not to say a word to Sarah or to her father until I had divorced Celia. But would Celia agree to a divorce? I was afraid to write her. If she learned where I was, she was liable to make trouble for me. It's a principle among today's men that the unjust are always in the right. Chutzpah is the very essence of modern man, and of the modern Jew as well. He has learned so assiduously from the Gentile that he now surpasses him. The truth is that the element of chutzpah was present even among the pious Jews. They have always been a stiff-necked and rebellious people. Well, there is a kind of chutzpah that is necessary, but I won't go into that now.

After I had decided to write a letter to Celia, I was overcome by a feeling of gloom and despair. I had wanted to break with my past, to try to forget, but now I would have to involve myself in it all over again. I slept badly and my dreams tormented me. I got up with the feeling that the game wasn't worth the candle, as the saying goes. No matter which way I turned, there were obstacles. Maybe it would really be better to put an end to my life, I mused. I don't know about others, but the notion of suicide had been with me since early in life. It seems that I even thought about it in cheder. I had always had the feeling that all my efforts were futile. I had heard from my parents that suicide was a terrible sin. But I didn't agree with them. Why shouldn't a person have the right to divest himself of his body and all its torments? When I studied the story of Hannah, who after losing her seven children committed suicide and still attained the world to come, this was a source of relief to me. If a suicide could attain paradise, then suicide could no longer be such a grievous offense. I know now that suicide is a sin. The suicide throws back God's greatest gift: free will. But there are circumstances when the person no longer has free will. There is a limit to suffering, too.

Yes, I got up in a melancholy mood. But despite this, I bathed and went off to the Sandzer study house. On the way, I stopped at a store displaying religious articles and bought a prayer shawl and phylacteries. The storekeeper looked at me in astonishment and asked, "Have you become a penitent?"

And I replied, "I want to be one."

I went to the Sandzer study house and met Reb Haim there. Seeing my prayer shawl and phylacteries, he remarked, "Well, you've come home!"

I started to pray and was assailed by painful thoughts. Even as I wound the thongs around my arm and kissed the fringes, the Evil Spirit harangued me: "You're acting out a farce. You know damn well that the phylacteries are hunks of leather torn from the skin of a cow. And that what you're reciting—the firstborn of an ass must be redeemed with a sheep, otherwise the ass's head must be chopped off—is a product of Phoenician idolatry. The cow did not deserve to have its hide stripped, nor did the sheep deserve to be sacrificed, nor did the firstborn ass deserve to lose its head. And this passage is like the whole Scripture and Talmud—stale, overgrown with the mold of centuries. Even what is written inside the phylacteries—you must love God with all your heart, soul, and being—has no justification. What did God do for us Jews that we should love Him so? Where is His love for us? Where was His love when the Nazis tortured Jewish children?''

I had already heard these arguments many times before, but I had never known how to answer them and—why bother to deny it?—I still don't know to this day. To get rid of the Glib One, I said, ''You're absolutely right, but since I don't have the courage to die, I must be a Jew. Why does it make less sense to put on a phylactery than to put on a tie, or stick a feather in one's hat? Even if Jewishness is nothing more than a game, I like this game better than football or baseball or the game of politics. Even if the Almighty is wicked, I'd rather speak to the unjust creator of the universe than to a scoundrel of the KGB. If God is no good, He is at least wise. But what are the wicked men? They are fools besides . . .''

I'm giving you my thoughts here to show you how hard it is for a modern person to turn back to God; how deeply the doubt and despair are rooted within us. I put on the prayer shawl and phylacteries and turned to pray, but Satan wouldn't let up on me for even a moment. When I recited: ''The Lord is good to all and His tender mercies are over all His works,'' Satan shouted: ''A damn lie! He is only good to a band of rich and powerful outcasts.'' When I recited: ''The Lord is nigh unto all them who call upon Him,'' Satan remarked: ''Didn't the pious Jews in the ghettos offer enough prayers to Him? And what did He have against the Jews during Chmielnitzky's times? According to your own theory, the Jewish people had attained their highest spiritual value then . . .''

That's how the saboteur within me wouldn't let up on me for even a moment. He wrangled with me while I was asleep and when I was awake. I had decided not to answer him altogether, to let him howl like a dog, as they say. He blasphemed, he laid waste everything and everybody, and I went on reciting my prayers. He sat within my brain like the gnat in Titus, but he still couldn't seal my lips. I said the Eighteen Benedictions—even if without fervor.

That day I wrote Celia the whole truth; naturally, in brief. I wrote her more or less the following: "I want to become a Jew like my father and grandfather. Help me to get a divorce."

I was sure that Celia wouldn't answer, or that she'd have me called in by some lawyer or the police. Since modern Jews want to be like Gentiles, who knows what the Jewish police are capable of?

In the days to come, I lived mechanically and like a condemned man. I prayed, I studied the Gemara, I ate in a kosher restaurant. When I told the restaurant proprietor that I was a vegetarian, he gave me a strange look and wanted to debate with me, but I was in no mood for it and I said, "I'll concede that you may be right, but do me a favor and give me what I want."

The man shrugged. "A man's wishes must be honored." And he gave me what I ordered.

I had more trouble with Reb Haim, who, when he heard that I was against the slaughter of animals, said, "That's not the way."

"Reb Haim, whoever has seen people being eaten can never again eat an animal," I said.

"One need not be more compassionate than the Almighty."

I realized that day that my vegetarianism would form a barrier between me and the Jews to whom I sought to get closer. They considered vegetarianism a worldly fad practiced by Gentiles and Jewish Gentiles. To them it indicated that I sought to be excessively saintly. One of the Sandzer Hasidim compared me good-naturedly to Esau, who according to the Talmud played the role of a overly pious man and asked his father how one gave a tithe of straw. The first night I ate at Reb Haim's house, it just so happened that his wife served a dairy meal. But Reb Haim wanted to invite me for the Sabbath, too, and I couldn't keep the secret from him any longer. When I told him that I did not eat fish or meat even on the Sabbath, he seemed shocked.

But I was determined to live the way I wanted and the way I understood. If this meant that I had to alienate myself from *all* people, it would be no tragedy either. If one was strong, one could endure this as well.

In the midst of all this, a letter arrived from Celia. It was a long letter, a kind of confession stretching over thirty pages. It's probably still lying somewhere among my papers, and believe me, this is a document. The gist of the letter was, first, that it was I who had led her to her evil ways. I had set a bad example for her. In this, she was entirely correct. Secondly, she wrote that she envied me my courage to break away from everything and everybody. There were times, she said, when she wanted to do the same, but unfortunately, she lacked the conviction, the faith, the courage. She told me that she was seeing the old professor and that he was anxious to divorce his wife and to marry her, Celia. She was ready to grant me the divorce and only sought a ''small settlement.'' Several of the pages had to do with business. I had abandoned everything without a care, but my partners had no wish to strip me of all I had. Also, Celia had hired a lawyer to see to our property.

I read the letter many times. It echoed the sentiments of a woman deeply depraved but not completely so. The essence of the letter was: ''Yes, we have lost our heritage, lost it forever. Nothing can be salvaged of it.''

15

Where was I? Oh, yes, I got the divorce from Celia; that is to say, she got the divorce in court and I sent her a Jewish divorce. The "small settlement" became a "big settlement." Celia and her lawyer grabbed as much as they could. When modern man marries a woman of his own kind, he falls into a viper's nest. Marriage for the modern person is a form of suicide. For a false smile and for a wife that other men have already had for free, a husband pays not only with his freedom but often with his life and health as well. She, the wanton female, demands that she be loved; she keeps on complaining that her husband doesn't love her enough. And she repays with betrayal. The nation that shed blood to free the slaves has transformed married men into slaves. The loose female has become the deity of America, and of modern man in a great portion of the world. The ancient idols were made of stone or gold, but today's idols are shrewd courtesans.

When I finally obtained the divorce, I felt like a slave who had been granted his freedom. My "good friend," the Evil Spirit, argued with me: "Now that you are free, don't get yourself involved in a new bondage. All roads are open to you now. You are still comparatively young, you are financially independent. The women in Tel Aviv will greet you with open arms, as would women in Paris, London, and the whole world. You can get many of them for a ticket to the theater, an outing in the country, or even for nothing. Now the time has come for you to live, not to rot away in the Sandzer study house browsing over a Gemara written by fanatics some two thousand years ago and praying to a God that doesn't exist."

That's how the Great Dialectician spoke; Satan, whose way it is to attach himself to every person in every era, in every situation. But I no longer had the slightest urge toward those fancy women in Tel Aviv or Paris. I literally felt a revulsion against them and their embraces. I had reached a stage wherein the modern woman with all her antics seemed like a cheap comedienne to me. Even her passion appeared false. Passion comes from the soul, and cold souls cannot love. The countless works published these days about sex, all the sexy plays and films, demonstrate one thing: that modern man is growing more and more impotent; that he needs more and more artificial incentives to stimulate him. Often I recall Celia and Liza complaining about their inability to achieve orgasm. Those who are preoccupied with sex twenty-four hours of the day, who read about sex, talk about sex, study sex, and breathe sex, can no longer enjoy sex when it comes to the actual deed. Those who talk smut all day cannot become aroused by a bold word or expression.

When the Evil Spirit changed his method and tried to prove to me that the whole female gender is wanton and vicious, I thought of my mother and grandmother. Everything that the Devil, who played the role of an anti-feminist now, said about women had no connection whatsoever to these old-fashioned women. They didn't enslave our grandfathers but helped them to earn a living. They were everything at once: wives, breadwinners, mothers. My father could have gone away for years without worrying that another man would take his place. Women in those days were often left without husbands at an early age, yet they never sinned with other men. There were instances when people strayed off the narrow path, but these were rare exceptions. Our mother and grandmothers bore the yoke of the Torah, of earning a livelihood, of raising children. They were saints, and they didn't have to brood about orgasms.

That's how my wife, Sarah, Reb Haim's daughter, was, and still is to this day. Many such decent Jewish daughters still live in the streets of Jerusalem and even of New York. They are like their mothers, grandmothers, and great-grandmothers before them. They bear on their narrow shoulders the remnants of our heritage. If they should ever be corrupted, God forbid, we would be finished as a people despite the strongest army, the greatest universities, the richest economy.

When I had supposedly decided that I wanted Sarah for my wife, my first thought was to try to have a flirtation with her, as such things go in novels. How could I, Joseph Shapiro, marry without being loved? I began to seek out opportunities to meet with Sarah and talk to her. When I happened to be in Reb Haim's house and she came in, I cast glances at her and even paid her compliments. Like all modern men, young or old, I considered myself an expert at evoking a woman's love. But I soon realized that the usual technique wasn't working here. When I looked at Sarah, she didn't look back. I paid her compliments, but she simply didn't respond. It seemed that this woman was instinctively aware of all the worldly tricks and was immune to them. I wanted to do her favors, to give her advice, but she needed neither favors nor advice. I heard her speaking to her mother and all the talk was about a pot, a spoon, a Sabbath meal.

The Evil One said to me: "That's how they are, these pious women—dried-up souls, frigid, without blood in their veins. To marry such a one would be like marrying a chunk of ice."

But I replied, "The whores are surely ice."

I had acquired that good chutzpah that I mentioned before.

The Good Spirit said to me: "Joseph, you don't snare such women with compliments. Talk to her father or send a matchmaker. That's how generations of Jews have gotten married."

"Well, and what about Jacob and Rachel? And the Song of Songs? And King David and King Solomon?" countered the Evil Spirit. "What about the boys and girl who used to dance in the vineyards in the Land of Israel and the girls would say, 'Lad, raise up your eyes'? . . . Weren't they good Jews, too? Must all Jews remain yeshiva boys or bashful wenches? And would Israel exist if all Jews remained like them? It would be torn to shreds in one day. One Jewish soldier is worth more to the welfare of the nation than are thousands of Hasid bigots. Israel needs soldiers, engineers, technicians, fliers. It is they who keep the country going. It is they who rescued the survivors of the Holocaust, All that the fanatics do is bleat their prayers. The girls that go into the army are a thousand times better than this Sarah whom you've picked out and her kind. Her going to the ritual bath and shaving her skull can't help anybody. While Jewish men and women were shedding their blood for the country, the Reb Haims and their daughters cowered like mice in the cellars and waited for miracles, ready to perish without the least resistance, like sheep led to the slaughter. Is this so exemplary? Is this so necessary? Are you one hundred percent sure that this is what the Almighty wants?"

Yes, when it suits the Evil Spirit, he can become a fervent Zionist, a burning patriot.

I listened as he argued further: "Thanks to the fact that worldly Jews build the land, fight, study, and work, those parasites from the Sandzer study house and their wives and children can practice piety and sponge off others. You are still a young and healthy man, Joseph Shapiro. You have experience in construction. You have capital, too. It's better that you help build up the country. There are enough Psalm reciters and breast-beaters in the land without you. If you must be an idealist, become a settler at a kibbutz. The girls there aren't like Celia and Liza. They marry for love, and most of them take their marriages seriously. They don't marry for money or for a career. If the love ends and you must part, it's no tragedy either. Nothing is forever. The institution of divorce existed among observant Jews, too. The idea that what God had joined together no man dare tear asunder stems from the New Testament and is the very opposite of Jewishness and of free will. The truth is that there is divorce in Meah Shearim, too."

What does it say in Proverbs? "There is that speaketh like the piercing of a sword." These are words that pierce you through and through, that wreck all your plans, that strip you spiritually bare. In those days and those weeks, I often heard such words. They upset and unnerved me so that I was left as if paralyzed. Words flung me from hot to cold, as it is said about the sinners in Gehenna. One minute I was ready to go to Reb Haim and propose to him that I marry his daughter, the next I was ready to drop everything and go to Tel Aviv, or even back to New York. I woke up at night and pictured the delights that I had once enjoyed with women and that I could still enjoy in the future. My rage against modern woman suddenly evaporated and I began to tally up her good points: her elegance, her refinement, her skill at facing up to the male and fanning his desire for her. Even promiscuity and deceit no longer seemed so awful to me. It was all part of the big sexual game, of the eternal drama between "him" and "her." I was amazed at how quickly my emotions swung from one extreme to the other.

I slept badly and got up late. I had completely lost the

urge to pray. Putting on the prayer shawl and phylacteries had become a burden. When I opened the Gemara and began to study about the laws of the Sabbath and about how to sacrifice the paschal lamb, I started to get sleepy. "It's not for you! Not for you!" the voice within me shouted.

Early one morning, I forgot (made myself forget) to go to pray. I went outside and took a stroll through the streets of the new Jerusalem. Houses were being built, hotels. The stores displayed more or less the same goods as in Tel Aviv or even New York. The streets here were wider and cleaner. Spring was coming.

Suddenly I heard somebody call my name: "Mr. Shapiro!" I looked around, and it was Priscilla, the girl I had met on the plane.

For a moment I considered not answering her and simply running away. But I ignored all my resolutions, went up to her, and we greeted each other. She put out her cheek to be kissed and I kissed it. One moment I was a Jew like my grandfather, and the next I was again a man from the twentieth century.

She said, "You're growing a beard?"

"Yes."

"It suits you. Why didn't you call? You promised you would."

I wanted to tell her that I had had enough of wantonness in New York and I didn't want any more of it in Jerusalem, but instead I offered the pretext that I had lost her telephone number. I could tell from her expression that she was glad to have bumped into me and that I wouldn't be able to rid myself of her so easily. We passed a café and she said, "Come on, let's have coffee."

"Don't go with her!" cried the Good Spirit, but my feet followed their own course. We were already sitting at a table, and a waitress came over to take our order. Priscilla ordered coffee and I tea. She wanted ice cream, too.

I said to her, "How is your professor?"

"Oh, Bill is just fine. He's already picked up a lot of Hebrew. He'll soon be talking like a Ṣabra. But to me, Hebrew sounds like Chinese. Luckily, everyone speaks English here. Everybody at the university, and the people in the street, too. Oh, with English and with dollars, you can make out anywhere."

And she smiled, gratified that she belonged to the nation of English and dollars. She told me that she had sublet someone's apartment. Its owner was a chemistry professor who had gone to study in Germany for a year.

I said, "How can a professor at the Jerusalem University, a Jew, go to a country full of Nazi murderers?"

And she replied, "Oh, you can't cling to such grudges forever. Many professors from Israel take courses in Germany."

She uttered the words "such grudges" as if they referred to some petty squabbles. The millions of murdered and tortured Jews, the gassed, the burned, the victims of sadistic experiments, concerned her as much as last year's frost. She felt at home in Jerusalem, and the professor who had sublet the apartment to her undoubtedly felt just as much at home in Bonn, Hamburg, or wherever he might be. He had probably already found himself a Fräulein there and she called him *Mein Schatz.*

I said to Priscilla, "How is that dark young man you sat next to on the way from Rome to Tel Aviv?"

"Oh, so you were spying on me? You disappeared somewhere and they gave me another seat. Imagine this: he is also a professor or a lecturer at the university. When he heard to whom I was going, he wouldn't leave my side."

I could tell from her eyes that she wanted to boast to me. That's the nature of adultery—it demands boasting. Among men and women both. This is actually true of all crimes. Many criminals have been caught and sentenced because they boasted. The reason for this is that crime actually provides little pleasure, not even physical pleasure. You have to enhance this pleasure through boasting. If someone envies him, this signifies to a person that he has really enjoyed something. I sat there listening and watching Priscilla's eyes gleaming. She spoke in a low, confidential tone. The name of the young man who sat next to her on the plane was Hans. He had come to Israel from Germany as a boy with his parents. Others had changed their names, but he had kept the name Hans. He was studying in Israel. Hebrew was, in a sense, his mother tongue. But he spoke excellent German, English, and French as well. He was studying psychology, anthropology, and who knows what else. A serious student. He had already been married, but he was divorced. It hadn't worked out between his wife and him. He had a little daughter of three. He was unusually intelligent and quite witty. He made puns that were simply ingenious. He wanted to become a diplomat.

"So you're having an affair, eh?"

Priscilla put a finger to her mouth.

"Really, I must be crazy," she said. "Otherwise I couldn't explain it myself. Bill is wonderful in every respect—good, tender, devoted. He is a marvelous lover besides. But he is a little too busy for me, and I have lots of time. Hans also has time. He's not as ambitious as Bill, and by nature he's a playboy. He has an apartment and he likes a drink. Yes, we do meet. I introduced him to Bill and he isn't at all jealous. Naturally, he doesn't know what we're up to, but he and Hans have become good friends. They hadn't met before I introduced them. Isn't that strange? A university is like a city. The professors don't even know each other."

"Must you have two men?" I asked her.

"I don't 'must,' but it's fun. Bill satisfies me completely, but it's convenient to meet Hans in the daytime when Bill is busy with his work. We have to be careful, but Jerusalem is a big city. He has the finest liquors at his place. Bill doesn't drink, but Hans likes cognac. We drink, then we forget ourselves. I beg you, don't look at me so sternly. I'm not killing anybody. Bill had other women, too, when I was in New York. He even introduced me to his former girlfriend. She is the wife of a psychology professor. How about you? How is it going for you here in the Holy Land?''

''Not bad.''

''Have you made friends,?'' she asked.

''Yes, 'friends.' ''

''Tell me about them. I like to hear such intimate things. After all, we spent some time together. If it hadn't suddenly become day, we might have—''

She didn't finish. Her eyes were amused. I wanted to test her and I said, ''You still owe me love.''

A smile spread over Priscilla's face. ''Owe? I owe nothing to no one. But I'll always remember those amazing two hours that I spent with you. An airplane is no place to make love. It's too difficult. Positively uncomfortable.''

''Would you come to my place?''

''Where are you staying?''

I told her where I lived and she said, ''I actually don't have the time. Two men are more than enough for me. Besides, I take courses in Hebrew and this takes up a lot of my time, too. But we don't have to become estranged. Every man who has so much as kissed me has a place in my heart. I never forget anything. Some time ago I thought of you as I was lying in bed. Isn't man a remarkable creature?''

''Yes, very.''

''I'm sure that you condemn me in your mind. You certainly label me a whore and other such things. But believe me, you're wrong. I'm true in my own fashion to Bill, and to Hans, too. I don't deceive either of them. I give each of them all of me. But the 'me' of a person is a complex thing. When I'm with Bill, I'm with him with my whole body and soul. And when I'm with Hans, then I'm all his, too. Each man has a different approach, a different style, and it's most intriguing to see how much individuality there can be in such a process as sex. Bill, for instance, doesn't talk when he makes love. He keeps his mouth shut. He wants it completely dark in the house, or at least partially so. He is serious through it all. If I say a word or make a joke, he says I'm disturbing him. Hans is just the opposite. He talks such nonsense that he keeps me in stitches the whole time. To him, the sexual process is tied in with humor. I like his lighthearted approach. I get more aroused by the fact that all this is taking place in such a holy city as Jerusalem. But I'm sure that God doesn't mind. To Him, the earth is nothing more than a speck of dust, and people a swarm of worms. Who would possibly care whether a worm copulated?"

"Worms don't deceive their mates."

"Well, I'm only trying to make a point. Actually there is no God. I'm completely convinced of this. To the Jews, Jerusalem is a holy city, and to the Arabs, Mecca is also holy."

"If there is no God and there are no divine laws, what can you have against Hitler? Why couldn't he do whatever he wanted to?"

"Oh, Hitler was a beast."

"If Hitler had won the war, he would be deified today. The professors would find a million justifications for him. They're writing many books about him as it is, and a whole literature is forming around him."

"Yes, he has definitely entered into world history. A professor of history can't skip over Hitler. He must also research the conditions that created him. Hans says that Hitler was impotent."

"Is that what he says? Probably he knows."

"Oh, he had a sweetheart, Eva Braun, but it may be that it was all platonic."

"Could you be Hitler's sweetheart?" I asked.

Priscilla's eyes filled with laughter. "You have such funny ideas."

"Wouldn't it be interesting to spend a night with him?"

"Oh, I never thought of him in that context," she said. "He's not my type at all."

"Nevertheless, if you were riding with him in an airplane in the dark and no one was looking, you'd probably be curious to find out how such a person made love."

"Oh, you're sarcastic today. No, Hitler is definitely not my type. I'd have sooner made it with Mussolini. They say that he had a thousand women. He sent out agents across all Italy to seek out victims for him. And he wasn't at all particular."

Priscilla took sips of coffee. She lit a cigarette and said, "Something has happened to you."

"Nothing has happened to me," I replied, "but something has happened to my people. A great tragedy. God chose us out of all the peoples and wanted us to avoid their abominations, but we often do the same as our persecutors. He keeps punishing and we keep sinning. The evildoers flog us, stab us, and burn us, yet at the same time many of us try to copy their ways. Within our time we were dealt the worst blow a people can receive, yet we learned nothing from it."

"Oh, I saw right away that you're in a strange mood," Priscilla said. "Were you there when God chose us? You get all your information from the Bible and the Bible is a book like all other books. Men wrote it, not God. I'm no Bible expert, but it's enough to read two pages to see that these are men's words, men's concepts. For the Christians, the New Testament is also the Bible, and for four hundred million Mohammedans, the Koran is the Bible. There is no proof," Priscilla went on, "that the Jews' sufferings were a punishment from Heaven. The Jews were a small nation and they caught it from the Egyptians, the Persians, the Babylonians, the Greeks, and the Romans. The other small nations assimilated and became part of the bigger nations, but the Jews were masochists. They liked to receive blows. I'm sure that the present experiment with Israel will not last long either. They're again surrounded by tens of millions of enemies, and your God will look on with the same indifference when Israel is destroyed as He did when the ghettos in Poland were being leveled. The fact is, I'm afraid this might happen tomorrow or the day after. Each time I hear the roar of a jet it seems to me it has started already."

That's what Priscilla said, and she looked at me with sharp reproof. Her gaze seemed to ask, "What can you say in reply to this? How can you be so sure that what I'm saying is not the whole, bitter truth?"

16

"*Priscilla*," I said, "*it may be that what you say* is *the bitter* truth. Neither you nor I were in Heaven. I'm not so pious yet that I don't nurse any doubts. But even if I knew there is no God, or there is a God but He is on Hitler's side, I would still refuse to go along with those who agree to murder, lies, falseness, theft, and such. If there is no God, or if God is amoral, then I want to serve that idol who is supposed to be moral, who loves the truth, who has compassion for people and animals. Decent Jews served this idol for four thousand years. For this idol, they went to the pyres."

"Is it worth going to a pyre for an idol?" Priscilla asked.

"Yes, Priscilla," I replied. "If millions of Germans sacrificed themselves for the idol Hitler, and so many millions of Russians and Jews sacrificed themselves for the idol Stalin, I'm ready to sacrifice myself—or at least to suffer— for the idol in whose name we received the Ten Commandments and the whole Torah. If it's already man's destiny to serve idols, then I want an idol that meets my requirements, rather than one who evokes revulsion in me twenty-four hours of the day."

"Why serve any idol at all?" Priscilla asked. "I don't serve anybody."

"Yes, you do serve. You gave up years to learn languages. You and your kind squander your lives for pleasures that are no pleasures at all. Your kind undergo operations to shorten your noses. You wage a hopeless war against growing old. Many people like you have lost their lives in the name of Communism, Nazism, or some other 'ism.' Every hollow slogan, every foolish theory demands its victims, and there is never any lack of volunteers to make the sacrifice. All the jails and hospitals are full of people who sacrificed themselves for a few dollars, for a woman, for a hazardous game, for a horse race, for revenge, for drugs, and for the devil knows what else. Every new invention demands countless new victims. The automobile has already killed millions of people. The airplane, too, is an angel of death. Alcohol kills millions of others. Thousands of women die of abortions. Countless men and women have suffered and died and continue to suffer from venereal disease. The 'idol' that I want to serve is an idol of life and of faithfulness. He demands no victims. He is not a Moloch. All he demands is that we don't build our happiness on the misfortune of another."

"That's morality, not religion."

"There's no such thing as morality without religion. If you don't serve one idol, you serve another. Of all the lies in the world, humanism is the biggest. Humanism doesn't serve one idol but all the idols. They were all humanists: Mussolini, Hitler, Stalin. Well, and what are the patriots in any of the countries? Hundreds of thousands of Englishmen perished to enable Victoria to bear the title of empress. A Napoleon sent millions to their deaths so that he could wear a crown on his head. The pious Jews, the *Talmud Jude,* never served any king or prince. They were driven to their deaths, but at least they didn't go of their own free will."

"Does this mean that you want to become a pious Jew like those who go around here with long gaberdines and earlocks?"

"Yes, exactly like them."

"Well, I wish you luck. But this is only a mood. It will last no more than a few days or, at the most, a few weeks."

"I'll never go back to being your kind of person anymore."

We said goodbye and we each went our own way. I was ashamed of myself for having lectured this way to her, but sometimes talking to others clarifies things for yourself. Yes, I was ready to become a Jew even if the Torah was a figment of the imagination and if there was no God.

That night, I told Reb Haim everything that had happened to me. I also told him that I wanted to marry his daughter.

I believe that this is more or less the story I wanted to tell you. After I got the divorce from Celia, I married Sarah. As you see, I let my beard and earlocks grow, I put on a long gaberdine, and once and for all I broke with everything that had to do with modern Jewry.

I don't want to mislead you that all this came easily to me. There were days when I wanted to leave Sarah and run back to Gehenna. There were nights when I couldn't close an eye, and tossed as if in a fever. Everyone knows that smoking cigarettes can cause cancer, but hundreds of millions still can't break themselves of this imaginary pleasure. Everyone knows that overeating leads to heart trouble, but millions of people still stuff themselves with all kinds of unhealthy foods. Everyone knows that Communism kills its adherents, but if Russia would make even the slightest gesture toward the modern Jews, many would revert to that idolatry with the same fervor as before. Maybe they've already taken down Stalin's picture in that kibbutz, but they still long for the Red idolatry. I say this because, although I knew for years that what I longed for was a deadly poison, I still longed for it. But as the saying goes, I had burned my bridges behind me.

As I said, I married Sarah, and she soon became pregnant. I have three children with her and the fourth is on the way. I've used up a good chunk of my money. I've lost some teeth and I haven't replaced them with false ones. What for? I neither want to nor do I have to appeal to anyone anymore. My wife doesn't have a full set of teeth either, but this doesn't make me love her any less or be unfaithful to her.

One of modern man's most inane passions is reading newspapers in order to keep up with the latest news. The news is always bad and it poisons your life, but modern man can't live without this poison. He must know about all the murders, all the rapes. He must know about all the insanities and false theories. The newspaper isn't enough for him. He seeks additional news on the radio or on television. Magazines are published that sum up all the news of the week, and the people reread what crime this or that evildoer has committed and what every idiot has said. The craze of politics has even seized our so-called orthodoxy. And as for the passion for money! If you read the orthodox press, you hear a single message trumpeting from every article and story: "Give money!" They need endless amounts of money to build yeshivas, to maintain—as they put it—Jewishness. It's an absolute lie. The big yeshivas, the bright classrooms, the good food, the examinations—this is all mimicry. There are already orthodox colleges in America or universities that teach the youth a little Torah and a lot of *goyishkeit*. The students are supposedly being trained to adjust to both worldliness and God. The fact is that once you are adjusted to the world, you can no longer be adjusted to God. Those children that prattle away in modern Hebrew, with its Sephardic pronunciation, will sooner or later read all the trashy books that are translated here. Hebrew must remain a holy tongue, not a language used in nightclubs.

I had told that wench Priscilla that the Jewish God was an "idol" to me. Maybe I meant it at the time. Faith is not an easy thing to acquire. Long after I had become a Jew with a beard and earlocks, I still lacked faith. But faith gradually grew within me. The deeds must come first. Long before the child knows that it has a stomach, it wants to eat. Long before you reach total faith, you must act in a Jewish way. Jewishness leads to faith. I know now that there is a God. I believe in His Providence. Whenever I'm troubled or a child of mine gets sick, I pray to the Almighty.

I won't boast to you that my faith is absolute. Maybe there is no such thing as total faith. But I believe more today than I ever have before. Darwin and Karl Marx didn't reveal the secret of the world. Of all the theories about creation, the one expounded in Genesis is the most intelligent. All this talk about primordial mists or the Big Bang is a wild absurdity. If someone found a watch on an island and said it had been made by itself or that it developed through evolution, he would be considered a lunatic. But according to modern science, the universe evolved all on its own. Is the universe less complicated than a watch?

I know what you want to ask me—if I am still interested in sex. Believe me, a pure, decent woman can provide a man more physical satisfaction than all the refined whores in the world. When a man sleeps with a modern woman, he actually gets into bed with all her lovers. That's why there are so many homosexuals today, because modern man is sleeping spiritually with countless other men. He constantly wants to excel in sex because he knows that his partner is comparing him to the others. This is also the cause of impotence, from which so many suffer. They've transformed sex into a marketplace with competitors. Today's man must convince himself that he is the greatest lover and that Casanova was a schoolboy in comparison. He tries to convince the female, too, but she knows better.

The female is in the same position. She knows that her husband has, and has had, many other women, and she wants to compete with them, to be smarter than they are, prettier than they are. Modern man has injected competition into areas where it does not belong. All modern life is a series of contests to determine who is tallest, biggest, strongest; able to perform better than the others. Today's female yearns to be the most beautiful creature on earth.

Among those Jews with whom I live, there are no big people or little people. One man spends more time with the Torah; another, reciting Psalms. One has more time to study, another must work for a living. No one compares, no one measures himself against the others, and the main thing is: there is no chasing after budgets. They've freed themselves of the worst human passion—the need to be rich.

I'd be a liar if I told you that it's all sweetness and light among us. There are bad people here, too. The Evil Spirit hasn't been liquidated. Even as I sit there and study the Gemara, I think idle thoughts more befitting a wastrel. A moment doesn't pass without temptations. Satan is constantly on the attack. He never gets tired. But I have linked myself to Jewishness with bonds that are hard to tear. These bonds are my beard, my earlocks, my children, and now—my age as well.

At times, the Evil One says to me: "What will happen, Joseph Shapiro, if you should die and there is no hereafter? You will be a pile of dirt, blind, mute, a stone, a blob of mud."

I hear him out, and I reply, "My mortality would not prove that God is dead and that the universe is a physical or chemical accident. I see a conscious plan and purpose in all being, in man and in animals as well as in inanimate objects. God's mercy is often hidden, but His boundless wisdom is seen by everyone, even if they call Him nature, substance, absolute, or by any other name. I believe in God, His Providence, and in man's free will. I have accepted the Torah and its commentaries because I am sure that there is no better choice. This faith keeps growing in me all the time."

Author's Note

This novel was first serialized in the *Jewish Daily Forward* between January and March 1973. It was published in book form in Israel by the Peretz Verlag a year or so later. Like other writers, I nurture the illusion that there exists at least one reader who follows everything I have published, even things I have said in interviews. This devoted reader might have read my conversation with Richard Burgin in the magazine section of *The New York Times*, upon my return from Stockholm in January 1979. As I remember, I then expressed ideas which may seem to be the opposite of what the protagonist of *The Penitent* is saying. In the novel, Joseph Shapiro continuously berates men and women who have forsaken God, the Torah, and the Shulhan Arukh, but in that interview I voiced a severe protest against creation and the Creator. I recall saying that although I believed in God and admired His divine wisdom, I could not see or glorify His mercy. I ended the interview by saying that, if I were able to picket the Almighty, I would carry a sign with the slogan UNFAIR TO LIFE! I also mentioned my unpublished essay, "Rebellion and Prayer, or The True Protestor."

This imagined reader of mine could well ask me, "Do you repudiate now what you said then? Have you finally made peace with the cruelty of life, and the violence of man's history?" My candid answer is that Joseph Shapiro may have done so, but I haven't. I'm still as bewildered and shocked by the misery and brutality of life as I was as a six-year-old child, when my mother read to me the tales of war in the Book of Joshua, and the bloodcurdling stories of the destruction of Jerusalem. I still say to myself that there isn't and there cannot be a justification either for the pain of the famished wolf or that of the wounded sheep. As long as we dwell in the body, vulnerable to all possible variations of suffering, no real cure can be found for the calamity of existence. To me, a belief in God and a protest against the laws of life are not contradictory. There is a great element of protest in all religion. Those who dedicate their lives to serving God have often dared to question His justice, and to rebel against His seeming neutrality in man's struggle between good and evil. I feel therefore that there is no basic difference between rebellion and prayer.

While I was brought up among extremists who thought and felt like that angry man, Joseph Shapiro, I cannot agree with him that there is a final escape from the human dilemma, a permanent rescue for all time. The powers that assail us are often cleverer than every one of our possible defenses; it is a battle which lasts from the cradle to the grave. All our devices are temporary, and valid only for one specific attack, not for the entire moral war. In this sense I feel that resistance and humility, faith and doubt, despair and hope can dwell in our spirit simultaneously. Actually, a total solution would void the greatest gift that God has bestowed upon mankind—free choice.

This book, like many of my other works, was translated into English by my nephew Joseph Singer, the son of my late brother and master, I. J. Singer, and edited by my good friend Robert Giroux with the editorial assistance of Lynn Warshow.

I often discussed with my brother the lack of dignity and the degradation of modern man, his precarious family life, his greed for luxury and gadgets, his disdain of the old, his obeisance before the young, his blind faith in psychiatry, his ever-growing tolerance of crime. The agonies and the disenchantment of Joseph Shapiro may to a degree stir a self-evaluation in both believers and skeptics. The remedies that he recommends may not heal everybody's wounds, but the nature of the sickness will, I hope, be recognized.

I.B.S.

About the Author

Isaac Bashevis Singer was born in Radzymin, Poland, in 1904 and grew up in Warsaw. He emigrated to the United States in 1935. Among his works are the auto-biographical memoir *In My Father's Court*, and the novels *The Family Moskat*, *The Magician of Lublin*, and *Enemies, A Love Story*. His short story collections include *Gimpel the Fool*, *Short Friday*, and *A Crown of Feathers*. On being awarded the Nobel Prize for Literature, he was cited for his "impassioned narrative art which, with roots in a Polish-Jewish cultural tradition, brings the universal human condition to life."

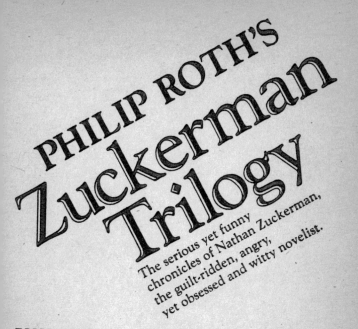

PHILIP ROTH'S Zuckerman Trilogy

The serious yet funny chronicles of Nathan Zuckerman, the guilt-ridden, angry, yet obsessed and witty novelist.